Our towns and cities:
the future

Delivering an urban renaissance

Presented to Parliament by
the Deputy Prime Minister and Secretary of State for the Environment, Transport and the Regions
by Command of Her Majesty
November 2000

Cm 4911

£28.00

Contents

Three other documents are being published with this White Paper:

- *The State of English Cities* by Brian Robson, Michael Parkinson, Martin Boddy and Duncan Maclennan, Department of the Environment, Transport and the Regions, Economic and Social Research Council Cities Programme.

- *Living in Urban England: Attitudes and Aspirations* by Jane Todorovic and Steve Wellington, Department of the Environment, Transport and the Regions.

- *The Government's Response to the Eleventh Report of the Select Committee on Environment, Transport and Regional Affairs: Proposed Urban White Paper*

All are available on the website www.detr.gov.uk

Foreword by the Deputy Prime Minister

How we live our lives is shaped by where we live our lives.

But wherever people live, they want the same things: jobs, a healthy economy, a decent home, good public services and an attractive and safe environment. North or south, urban or rural, the parts of our country – though different – are inextricably intertwined and interdependent. People also want to have a say in what happens in their community and to shape their own future.

Our guiding principle is that people must come first. Our policies, programmes and structures of governance are based on engaging local people in partnerships for change with strong local leadership. This inclusive approach is at the heart of our work on tackling social exclusion, and is central to achieving sustainable economic growth. And it's the approach which underlies both this White Paper and our parallel White Paper on rural communities.

As Lord Rogers, the chairman of the Urban Task Force, says, people make cities but cities make citizens. The quality of life for this and future generations depends not just on how we live and work together, but also on the state of our towns and cities. An urban renaissance is vital.

Britain has some of the best towns and cities in the world, containing famous historical and cultural centres, dynamic commercial areas, pleasant suburbs and leading seats of learning and research. But in the twenty years since the last Urban White Paper, many of our towns and cities have suffered from neglect, poor management, inadequate public services, lack of investment and a culture of short-termism.

Previous governments failed to stem urban decline because they only addressed part of the problem, and ignored the underlying causes. Often, they forgot that urban policies are not just about bricks and mortar, but about improving the prosperity and quality of life for the people who live there. Towns and cities need to be looked at as a whole in an integrated way. Good transport, for example, is not just important for the economy: it is also a key public service which contributes to the social well being of an area. Housing policies also have a powerful impact on local services, particularly health and education. In contrast to the past, we are adopting long-term policies which address economic, social and environmental needs together.

There have been real improvements in urban living over the past three years. Under Labour's New Deal unemployment in our inner-cities has fallen, the Working Families Tax Credit and the minimum wage are making work pay for millions of people on low incomes, programmes such as Excellence in Cities and Sure Start are helping to transform city education, health care has improved, crime rates are falling, and for the first time in a generation we are seeing a revitalisation of our town and city centres.

We have already provided extra money for key services and we will increase public spending year on year over the next 3 years to support community driven regeneration. By 2003/04 there will be an extra £10.4 billion a year for education, £13.7 billion for healthcare, £4.2 billion for transport, £1.6 billion for housing and £2.7 billion for criminal justice. We have also announced a comprehensive package of fiscal measures worth £1 billion over the next five years to encourage private investment for urban renewal. Our economic policies meanwhile have created a climate of stability.

We recognise that more needs to be done especially in the most disadvantaged areas where previous efforts have failed to reduce inequalities. In this White Paper we are committing ourselves to take further action.

The quality of the urban environment is crucial, and we are determined to improve the standard of urban planning, design and architecture. But we recognise that this is not, on its own, sufficient. We are determined to ensure that policies link together in a sustainable way to provide services and opportunities that will make people from across the social specturm want to live, as well as work, in our cities.

We know that an urban renaissance will not be achieved and sustained without the direct engagement of local people. So our policies will empower communities to determine their own future with support and co-ordinated action at the neighbourhood, local, regional and national levels.

This White Paper explains how our towns and cities can function as economic powerhouses, helping to achieve the Government's core objective of increasing sustainable growth and employment for all and bringing benefits not just to their own population but to the surrounding region. It also targets those areas that are striving to renew their economic identity and which are seeking to take full advantage of the rapid growth in the new industries.

We have set tough but achievable targets for the delivery of our policies and provided all those involved with the tools and resources to bring about sustainable change.

Our aim is to make urban living a positive experience for the many, not the few; to bring all areas up to the standard of the best; and to deliver a lasting urban renaissance.

John Prescott, Deputy Prime Minister

Summary

People make cities but cities make citizens

Lord Rogers of Riverside

Making our towns and cities places for people

1. We have a lot to be proud of in our towns, cities and suburbs. We have famous historical and cultural centres; dynamic commercial areas; pleasant suburbs; and seats of learning and research that command respect the world over. We want to build on success.

2. The challenges we face include:

- social changes with people living longer, having fewer children and many more living alone. As a result we may need to accommodate up to 3.8 million extra households by 2021;

- encouraging people to remain in, and move back into, our major towns and cities, both for the benefit of our urban areas and to relieve the pressure for development in the countryside;

- tackling the poor quality of life and lack of opportunity in certain urban areas;

- addressing the weak economic performance of some parts of our towns and cities and enabling all areas to compete successfully for jobs and investment in the global marketplace; and

- reducing the impact which urban living has on the environment, making sustainable choices practical and attractive.

3. The pace of change – economic, technological, environmental and social – is both a challenge and an opportunity. It requires a clear vision and effective action. Our approach is encapsulated in the following vision, which is at the heart of the White Paper.

A new vision of urban living

Our vision is of towns, cities and suburbs which offer a high quality of life and opportunity for all, not just the few. We want to see:

- **people shaping the future** of their community, supported by strong and truly representative local leaders;

- people living in **attractive, well kept towns and cities** which use space and buildings well;

- good design and planning which makes it practical to live in a **more environmentally sustainable** way, with less noise, pollution and traffic congestion;

- towns and cities able to **create and share prosperity**, investing to help all their citizens reach their full potential; and

- **good quality services** – health, education, housing, transport, finance, shopping, leisure and protection from crime – that meet the needs of people and businesses wherever they are.

This urban renaissance will benefit everyone, making towns and cities vibrant and successful, and protecting the countryside from development pressure.

People first

4.   Towns and cities exist to serve people's needs. Our approach recognises that:

- **no two places are the same.** Communities have different needs, different strengths and different aspirations. There can be no 'one-size-fits-all' approach; strategies must be tailored to each area and the people who live there;

- **people have a right to be involved in deciding how their town or city develops.** Real, sustainable change will not be achieved unless local people are in the driving seat right from the start. Successful cities are founded on participative democracy; and

- **everybody should be included.** This is both a mark of a decent society and plain good sense as a society which allows some to be excluded loses the benefit of their contribution.

Partnership and integration

5.   This White Paper commits us to working with local people, councils, regional bodies, businesses and voluntary and community organisations. The energy and effort of all concerned will reap greater rewards through genuine partnership.

6.   We also have to bring together economic, social and environmental measures in a coherent approach to enable people and places to achieve their economic potential; bring social justice and equality of opportunity; and create places where people want to live and work. These issues are interdependent and cannot be looked at in isolation. For instance, there are close links between housing, health and education. That is why moving towards more mixed and sustainable communities is important to many of our plans for improving the quality of urban life.

Local and regional leadership

7.   This White Paper builds on our programme for modernising local government. We will equip councils so that they can both deliver good quality services and offer strong, representative leadership.

8.   Each community affects and is affected by what happens in the wider region. Strategic planning for the region is essential. The new Regional Development Agencies have already made a major contribution to regeneration and we are now giving them increased resources and greater budgetary freedom.

Resources to make a difference

9.   This year's Spending Review provided substantial extra resources for all key service areas. By 2003/04 an extra £33 billion a year will be made available on top of a baseline of £106 billion.

Extra resources in 2003/04

	baseline £ billion 2000/01	increase £ billion by 2003/04	average annual real % increase
Education	38.8	10.4	5.4
Health	45.3	13.7	6.1
Transport	4.9	4.2	20.0
Housing	3.0	1.6	12.0
Criminal justice	12.5	2.7	4.1
Leisure, culture, sport	1.0	0.2	4.3

Criminal Justice data: England and Wales
All other data: England

10.   The increased resources are backed by challenging targets set out in Public Service Agreements. For the first time these include 'floor targets' specifying the minimum standard to be achieved in all areas, thus ensuring that adequate resources are allocated to deprived areas. We are also piloting local Public Service Agreements with local authorities.

Key steps towards renaissance

11.   Working with local people and regional and local partners, our strategy is to make all urban areas places for people by:

- getting the design and quality of the urban fabric right;

- enabling all towns and cities to create and share prosperity;

- providing the quality services people need; and

- equipping people to participate in developing their communities.

12.   The strategy is supported by measures announced in Spending Review 2000 and other major policy statements, as well as new ones introduced in this White Paper.

Getting the design and quality of the urban fabric right

13. This means well-designed places that put people first and make efficient use of the available space and environmental resources. It is the vision expressed in the report of Lord Rogers' Urban Task Force.

Better planning and design

14. We want to create places that:

- provide attractive homes;

- have plenty of good quality public spaces in which people feel safe;

- allow people easy access to local shops, schools, health and leisure facilities on foot or bike; and

- are sustainable and well served by efficient and reliable public transport.

15. We will use the planning system to full effect. We also need to strengthen the pool of skilled professionals able to take this agenda forward.

Bringing brownfield land and empty buildings back into constructive use

16. At present these are wasted assets. We have put in place measures to:

- exploit their potential so that they contribute to the quality of urban life, rather than detract from it; and

- use previously developed land to prevent urban sprawl and pepper-pot developments.

Looking after the existing urban environment well

17. The vast majority of the current urban fabric will still be with us in 30 years time. We must care properly for what we have by:

- tackling litter, graffiti, vandalism and noise;

- maintaining and improving streets and buildings; and

- making sure parks, playgrounds and other public spaces are safe and attractive places.

Key measures

- Comprehensive **£1 billion package of national taxation measures** to increase investment in urban areas including plans to introduce:

  - **an exemption from stamp duty for all property transactions in disadvantaged communities;**

  - **accelerated payable tax credits for cleaning up contaminated land;**

  - **100 per cent capital allowances for creating 'flats over shops' for letting;**

  - **package of VAT reforms to encourage additional conversions of properties for residential use;**

- Consultation on options for funding Town Improvement Schemes and for a Local Tax Reinvestment Programme.

- New **planning policy guidance** putting urban renaissance at the heart of the planning system; and new drive to implement planning policy on housing.

- Review of **planning obligations** system and commitment to bring forward new legislation on **compulsory purchase** as soon as possible.

- A third **Millennium Community** (four more to follow) and up to 12 more **Urban Regeneration Companies**.

- Comprehensive programme to improve the quality of **parks, play-areas and open spaces**, including the introduction of a new Green Flag Awards scheme to encourage and recognise excellence.

Enabling all towns and cities to create and share prosperity

18. Each area needs to identify its future role in the regional and national economy and develop and implement a strategy that builds on its strengths and tackles its weaknesses. Our policies and programmes provide the building blocks.

19. We need to promote a culture of enterprise and innovation and encourage private investment.

20. In particular we must ensure that everyone has the education and training they need and access to jobs so that they can achieve their full potential and share in and contribute to the nation's wealth.

21. We must also provide an efficient, reliable and safe transport system to contribute to business efficiency and improve people's access to jobs and services.

Key measures

- Giving the **Regional Development Agencies** a strengthened focus with significant increases in funding and greater budgetary flexibility.

- Promoting a culture of **innovation and enterprise** across society by services such as the Small Business Service and programmes like the Phoenix Fund, and the Higher Education Innovation Fund.

- Exploring a range of proposals for reforming the tax system to provide better incentives for boosting **private investment** in enterprise, particularly in under-invested areas.

- Creating the conditions for **e-commerce**. for example through launching UK online.

- Providing **employment opportunities** for all through enhancement of New Deal programmes and tax and benefit reforms to make work pay.

- Equipping people with **skills** through the new Learning and Skills Councils and other programmes, including the University for Industry.

- Investing £180 billion in a 10 year plan for **transport** to modernise and up-grade our transport networks.

Providing good quality services that meet people's needs

22. We have established the policies and programmes we need to deliver a step change in all the areas that are essential to quality of life – education, health, jobs, housing, transport, crime reduction, culture, leisure and sport.

23. We are committed to narrowing the gap between deprived areas and elsewhere. We will shortly be setting out specific measures in an action plan for neighbourhood renewal.

Key measures

- Raising **educational attainment and employment** opportunities:
  - expansion of Excellence in Cities education programme and Sure Start;
  - New Deal for Schools and free early education for 66% of 3 year olds in areas of greatest need; and
  - 40 new action teams for jobs.

- **Improving health** through a major expansion of investment in the health service across a wide range of programmes.

- Major investment to deliver the proposals in the **housing** green paper – *Quality and Choice: a Decent Home for All* – including starter homes for key workers.

- **Cutting crime** through an enhanced crime reduction programme and crime reduction partnerships.

- Promoting **culture, leisure and sporting activity** through new creative partnerships for schools and by putting in place the Spaces for Sports and Arts Scheme.

Equipping people to participate in developing their communities

24. We are setting out better ways of engaging local people in finding solutions, drawing on the experience and expertise many have already developed.

Key measures

- **Supporting individuals and communities to take their ideas forward**, for example, through New Deal for Communities, community chests and the Community Champions initiative.

- Introducing **Local Strategic Partnerships** which will give communities a clear voice in the development of the Community Strategy for their areas.

- A **Neighbourhood Renewal Fund** of £800m over 3 years.

- Consultation on a **New Opportunities Fund** initiative to enable communities to fund their ideas for improving the **local environment**.

---

25. Everyone has a part to play in delivering the urban renaissance. Government at all levels must lead and enable, working in partnership with local communities, the voluntary sector and businesses.

- There will be a new focus for urban policy at the heart of the Government. This will bring in a wide range of experience and help the Government develop and implement the new policies and programmes.

- Local and regional partners will need to ensure that each town and city has a clear vision of how to create its own renaissance. These should bring together all the interrelated aspects. The role of Local Strategic Partnerships will be central.

- Public and private bodies, local groups and individuals can transform their areas through projects of all scales, whether a neighbourhood green space, a major area needing an Urban Regeneration Company or a new development.

26. We will monitor progress closely. There will be a first major stocktaking in 2002 when Ministers will host an Urban Summit. In 2005 we will publish a major report on the state of our towns and cities.

A long term commitment to action

27. This is an ambitious long term programme of change and development in our towns and cities. If places are for people then people must help make the places. The Government has set out its commitment. It will lead the way forward but action will ultimately depend on everyone contributing to change whether as individuals in their own street and neighbourhood, as investors and businesses in shaping the economy of their city, or as local representatives creating the vision for their city.

Towns and cities today

Contents

Introduction

1.1 This White Paper and the parallel Rural White Paper *Our Countryside: the Future – A Fair Deal for Rural England* are about the quality of life in the communities in which we live.

1.2 Wherever we live, in towns, cities, suburbs or rural areas, we want the same things: jobs, a healthy economy, decent houses, good public services and an attractive and safe environment. In most areas there is much that is good that we want to preserve and enhance. In some areas there are major problems – a poor environment, a failing local economy, inadequate services and serious social problems. Other areas have less serious problems. These need to be addressed so that all can share in and contribute to our growing prosperity as a nation.

1.3 Wherever we live we face the challenge of adapting to a fast changing world. We are living longer, having children later and more of us are living alone. Our economy has changed radically with the role of manufacturing declining and the growth of service, new technology and creative industries. We need to compete on a global scale for jobs and investment. The challenge of protecting our environment locally and globally becomes ever more urgent. We are a densely populated country in which people are continuing to leave our major conurbations, with major implications both for urban areas and for the countryside and rural communities.

1.4 The approach that underlies our two White Papers is the same: people must come first. Our policies, programmes and structures of governance are about engaging local people in a partnership for change and enabling communities to take a decisive role in their own future. This is the same approach that underpins our work on tackling social exclusion and it is central to achieving sustainable economic growth.

1.5 The two White Papers deal largely with England. For the rest of the UK most of the issues they address are matters for the devolved administrations.

Urban and rural

1.6 There are real differences between rural and urban communities but what binds them together is greater than the differences. Each has much to offer the other. They are closely and inextricably inter-related. The economic, social and environmental influence of our towns and cities stretches well beyond their boundaries into the surrounding regions. Whether we live in rural or urban areas our livelihood and well-being depend on both. We spend our leisure time in both and value the contributions each makes to our quality of life. Improving the quality of urban life so that people want to stay in and return to the central areas of our cities and major conurbations is important not just to the health of those areas. It is also vital if we are to relieve the pressure for development in the countryside and preserve the essential qualities of rural communities.

1.7 Towns, cities and suburbs are where most of us live our daily lives. Despite this England is physically a rural country. 80% of us live in cities and towns of over 10,000 people but these only cover some 7% of our land. (Chart 1 and Map 1). We have much fine countryside. Agriculture has shaped our valued landscapes. We must preserve this irreplaceable national resource.

1.8 We have much to be proud of in our towns and cities. We have historic towns and cities that are famous the world over. We have a priceless architectural heritage. We have fine squares, elegant terraces and a legacy of great civic buildings. We have pleasant suburbs and good parks and public places. Many of our towns show what can be achieved in the modern age.

1.9 But we should not be complacent. Not everyone lives in the more successful towns and cities. Many people live in areas which have physical problems of dereliction or where communities have been damaged by deprivation. We want everyone to enjoy the quality of life of the best.

Chart 1 Proportion of land used and proportion of population accommodated by settlement size

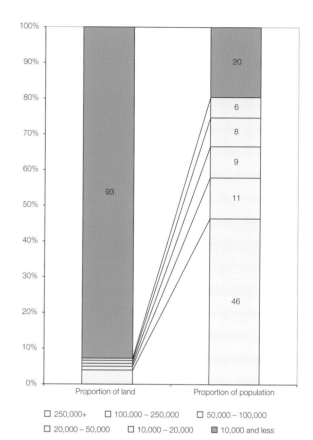

- □ 250,000+
- □ 100,000 – 250,000
- □ 50,000 – 100,000
- □ 20,000 – 50,000
- □ 10,000 – 20,000
- ■ 10,000 and less

Source: 1991 Census and DETR

Quality urban design in Sheffield
(Photograph: Richard Townshend)

Map 1 Urban Areas with a population exceeding 10,000

Produced by the GIS Unit, PLUS5, DETR, using the 1991 DETR Urban Area Boundaries and the Ordnance Survey 1994 Boundary Line data, with the sanction of the Controller of HM Stationery Office. Licence no.GD272671.
Crown Copyright Reserved 2000.

Quality urban design in Birmingham
(Photograph: Richard Townshend)

Towns, cities and suburbs

1.10   Our towns and cities are diverse in character, reflecting their history, scale, recent economic fortunes and location. Each contains many contrasting areas. The way forward needs to be grounded in an understanding of the past, the present and the pressures for future change. The analysis in the *State of English Cities* (which we are publishing alongside this White Paper) gives us an understanding of that diversity and change through identifying and analysing differing types of area, ranging from Inner London through to remote rural areas. Over 40% of us live in London, the conurbations and the bigger cities (Chart 2). Each of those major urban areas has a potentially wide influence.

1.11   London stands apart as a city competing in a global context especially in financial and cultural activities, and with a concentration of political institutions. It is the second most densely populated region in Europe. Despite having the highest GDP per head of any English city it also has one of the lowest rates of overall employment and contains one of the largest concentrations of deprived areas. London's impact extends far beyond its own boundaries. It influences the wider south east region and national economic growth.

Chart 2 Population by area type: detailed classification

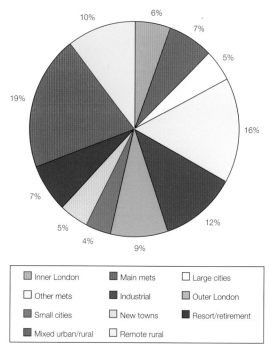

Legend:
- Inner London
- Main mets
- Large cities
- Other mets
- Industrial
- Outer London
- Small cities
- New towns
- Resort/retirement
- Mixed urban/rural
- Remote rural

Source: based on 1998 mid year population estimates

Chart 3 Employment rate of working age population by area type

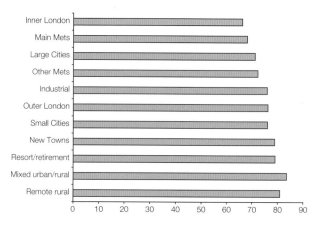

Source: Labour Force Survey; 1998/99 local area database

1.12 The major conurbations such as Birmingham and Manchester and some of the major freestanding cities such as Nottingham are at the core of their regions and influence the overall prosperity of the region. They are often centres for specialist professional services (law, medicine, finance), for learning and for cultural and sporting facilities which are of regional or even national importance. They compete on a European scale.

1.13 Other freestanding cities and smaller towns such as Ipswich or Blackburn are sub-regional centres of employment, education, culture and services. Some are prosperous and will be subject to development pressures. Others, including seaside resorts and towns formerly dependent on one main industry, have significant deprivation and slower economic growth.

Centres and Suburbs

1.14 There are still more complex patterns within our towns and cities. In *Living in Urban England: Attitudes and Aspirations* (which we are publishing alongside this White Paper) we clarify the differences between the core, inner, suburban and outer areas of towns and cities. Only 9% of us live in the centres of towns and cities at a fairly high density of around 85 people per hectare (Chart 4). Most of us live in places that we think of as suburbs, ranging from the older inner suburbs through the typical interwar and postwar suburbs, comprising mainly semi-detached houses, to more recent development at modest density.

1.15 The physical pattern of settlement varies around the country. Many of the main cities have a simple pattern of suburbs of gradually decreasing density surrounding the core. In the West Midlands and some other areas the suburbs are adjacent to rather than surrounding the core (Map 2).

Chart 4 Percent of population by urban, suburban and rural areas

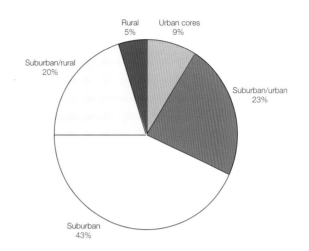

Source: Based on analysis from Living in Urban England: Attitudes and Aspirations, DETR, 2000

1.16 These overall patterns are the product of the complex interaction between natural growth, the impact of changing transport, people's preferences and planning. For example many of the centres of our cities and towns were reconfigured, mainly during the 1960s and 70s, to make way for road schemes and urban renewal built around motor transport. This has not only destroyed the physical appearance of some of those city centres but has also caused the severance and dislocation of communities and higher levels of pollution, congestion and noise. Although subsequent planning decisions have improved this situation, in many cases the scars remain.

Map 2 Classification of wards in the West Midlands area

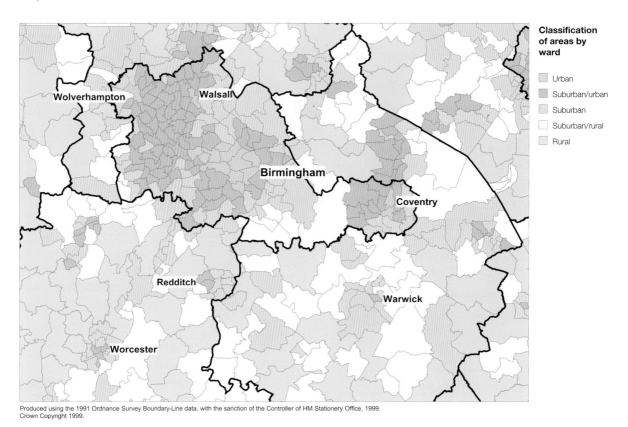

Classification of areas by ward

- Urban
- Suburban/urban
- Suburban
- Suburban/rural
- Rural

Produced using the 1991 Ordnance Survey Boundary-Line data, with the sanction of the Controller of HM Stationery Office, 1999.
Crown Copyright 1999.

The fabric of our towns and cities

1.17   The physical fabric of our towns and cities is dominated by housing. This is a major inheritance: since 1850 25 million homes have been built or provided through conversion. In that time we have lost four million homes to demolition or other uses. The fabric reflects over 150 years of residential building and the changing needs and fashions of different periods have produced the variety of homes in which we live. Chart 5 shows the age and construction type of the current housing stock. Over 60% of homes are more than 35 years old. 81% are houses; 50% are detached or semi-detached houses.

1.18   There are contrasts with other countries. In France and Germany around 50% of the homes are houses. In America there is a higher proportion of flats than in England.

Diverse people

1.19   Our cities are home to many communities. A wide variety of minority ethnic communities live mainly in our conurbations and cities (Chart 6). Over two-thirds of our minority ethnic communities live in London and the three large metropolitan areas in the West Midlands, Greater Manchester and West Yorkshire.

1.20   This diversity is a great strength for these cities, providing a cosmopolitan culture which is an important part of the attractiveness of cities. It enables, for example, business to draw on people with an international culture and understanding.

Chart 5 Age and type of current housing stock in England

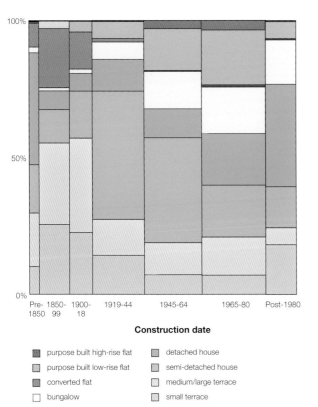

Construction date

Legend:
- purpose built high-rise flat
- purpose built low-rise flat
- converted flat
- bungalow
- detached house
- semi-detached house
- medium/large terrace
- small terrace

Source: English House Condition Survey 1996, DETR, 1998

Chart 6 Patterns of settlement for different ethnic groups

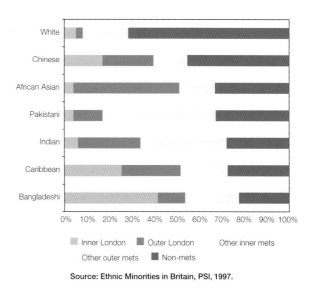

Legend:
- Inner London
- Outer London
- Other inner mets
- Other outer mets
- Non-mets

Source: Ethnic Minorities in Britain, PSI, 1997.

The economic role of towns and cities

1.21   The economy relies on the economic performance of our towns and cities. The Urban Task Force reported that urban areas provide 91% of national output and 89% of jobs. Many towns and cites have vibrant commercial and industrial areas that are powerhouses for the surrounding regions. They are centres of expertise and professional skills in areas such as finance, law and medicine. Some are seats of learning and research that have an international reputation.

1.22   Preserving and strengthening such assets is vital as we live in an increasingly competitive world. If we are to attract and retain jobs and investment we must offer the facilities, the skilled and adaptable workforce, the public services and an urban environment to match the best in the world.

Culture, leisure and sport

1.23   Culture, leisure and sport are becoming increasingly important both as components of our quality of life and as economic sectors in their own right. With increasing prosperity, changing lifestyles and lengthening lifespans we have more free time and resources to devote to non-work activities. Reflecting this and the relative decline in the importance of manufacturing industry, culture, leisure and sport have become a more and more significant part of the economy.

1.24   Our towns and cities already have much to offer here and the potential for significant expansion. They have theatres, concert halls, art galleries and museums that are regional if not national resources. Some of them are famous throughout the world. These and the historic areas already attract millions of tourists.

Perceptions of towns and cities

1.25   This pen picture of our towns and cities today records the physical facts. But how people view towns and cities is equally important. *Living in Urban England: Attitudes and Aspirations* (which we are publishing with this White Paper) summarises what we know from recent surveys.

19

1.26 Over 85% of residents say that they are satisfied with the area in which they live and the proportion of people identifying problems has decreased in recent years. But within that overall satisfaction there are differences between areas and evidence of concern about many of the key features of urban living. We return to this in Chapter 2.

Building on diversity and strength

1.27 Government has a key part to play both in preserving and enhancing success and in intervening in those areas of our towns and cities which are manifestly not working for the benefit of the people who live in them.

1.28 The rich and diverse patterns of our towns and cities requires a complex range of policy approaches. What may be the best policy to revitalise our inner cities or renew some of our worst estates is likely to be completely inappropriate for suburban areas. What may be necessary to maintain and improve our suburban residential areas would be completely inappropriate for our industrial and commercial areas. Government policies must be tailored to meet the particular needs of particular areas.

1.29 Government must provide a clear lead and establish a vision for the future of our towns and cities. The vision must recognise the complexity of our urban areas and the dynamic nature of our towns and cities. It must address the key issues that have shaped their recent past in order to ensure a healthy and sustainable future which complements and reinforces the revival in the countryside. The next chapter discusses these issues.

Towns and cities: issues and vision

Contents

Introduction

2.1   Towns and cities grow, survive and prosper because they attract and retain people and businesses. We need towns, cities and suburbs which offer a high quality of life and opportunity for everyone. This White Paper sets out a framework, polices and programmes to achieve that goal. This chapter discusses the five distinct but closely interrelated issues which derive from the legacy we have in our towns and cities and from the pressures they face:

- there are likely to be up to 3.8 million extra households to be accommodated by 2021;

- people and jobs have left our major towns and cities for the suburbs, smaller towns and rural areas;

- in some parts of our towns and cities the quality of life is poor and there is a lack of opportunity;

- the economic performance of some urban areas has been poor and has adversely affected the wider region; and

- these and other aspects of the way we live can damage the environment locally and globally.

2.2   Understanding these issues and their relationships will enable us to set out a practical vision for the future of our towns and cities.

The demand for homes

2.3   In 1996 England had a population of 49 million. That figure is projected to grow slowly – by about 3.4 million people or 7% over the 25 years to 2021. The growth in the number of households is projected to be much larger. There were some 20 million households in England in 1996. This is projected to grow to 24 million by 2021, an increase of 3.8 million or 19%. This is the continuation of a very long run trend over the last century for the size of our households and families to reduce. As a result the number of households has grown at a much faster rate than the population (Chart 1).

Chart 1 Demographic Trends 1901 to 2021 England

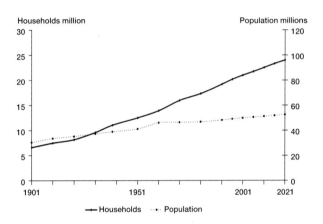

Source: DETR

2.4   The biggest increase – some 70% or 2.7 million – is in the number of single-person households. This is a combination of young people living alone, more people who are divorced or unmarried and a growing proportion of older people. By 2021 35% of all households will be one person living alone (compared with 29% in 1996) and about 50% are projected to be married or co-habiting couples (compared with 57% in 1996) – see Chart 2.

Chart 2 Household composition: England: 1971, 1996 & 2021

1971

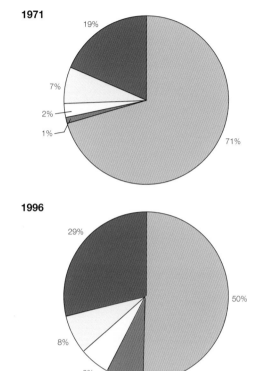

1996

2021

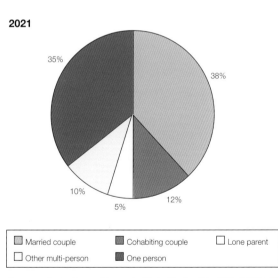

Source: Projections of households in England to 2021, DETR, 1999

The consequences of the projected growth in households

2.5 The household projections are based on previous trends. No one can predict with certainty how many households will exist in 20 years time. Nor are the projections an estimate of the number of additional homes which will have to be provided. But the implications of accommodating such projections would be stark without the new policies we have put in place to plan for future housing needs. As the Urban Task Force noted in its report:

- if we were to build 3.8 million new homes at the prevailing average density for new development, they would cover an area larger than Greater London; and

- if we continue to build 45% of the new homes on greenfield land at prevailing average densities for greenfield development, they would cover an area bigger than Exmoor.

The exodus from our towns and cities

2.6 The population changes and movements over the last half-century have been complex. There have been three factors at work:

- the 'natural growth' in the urban population as a result of births exceeding deaths as people live longer;

- the flows into and out of our towns and cities from and to other places in the UK. The net migration figure is the difference between two much larger figures. For example, between 1991 and 1997, for every five people that moved out of our conurbations, four moved in; and

- a significant net movement of people into our conurbations from abroad.

2.7 The effect of these factors has changed over the last fifty years.

- Between 1951 and 1981 the overall population of Britain grew by just over 9%. Many of our cities and towns also grew over this period – particularly in the south of the country. But our major conurbations lost 10% of their population and, while the rate slowed over the 80s, the decline continued.

- However, between 1991 and 1997 the population of our conurbations grew. This was as a result of natural growth and movements from abroad exceeding the net outward migration within the UK.

- Other towns and cities also grew between 1991 and 1997, some at a similar rate to the conurbations but others – particularly New Towns – have had a higher rate of population growth.

- Throughout the last 50 years the net migration *within* the UK has been consistently outwards from our conurbations. Even during the period from 1991 to 1997 the net exodus out of English conurbations averaged 90,000 a year.

Table 1 Ranking of net out-migration rates from conurbations, 1990/91, for six social groups

Social Group	Greater London	Greater Manchester	Merseyside	South Yorks	Tyne & Wear	West Midlands	West Yorks
Professional	3	1	1	2	1	2	1
Managerial	1	2	5	5	2	1	3
Technical	5	3	2	1	3	3	2
Other non-manual	6	4	4	3	4	4	4
Skilled manual	2	5	6	6	6	5	5
Other manual	4	6	3	4	5	6	6

Ranking: 1 for highest rate of out-migration and 6 for lowest rate
Source: *Outward migration: a threat to urban development?* By Tony Champion in ESRC's Cityscape, Autumn 1999

Chart 3 Population Trends By Type of Settlement

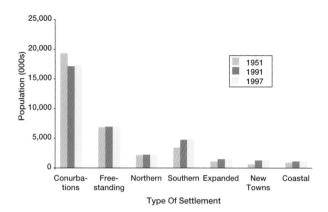

Source: The State of English Cities, DETR 2000

2.8　More detailed studies of the population movements suggest that there has been a cascade (Chart 4) with people, and families in particular, leaving the centres of the larger urban areas and heading for the suburbs, smaller towns and rural areas. At the same time those living in suburbs have tended to move further out. In most conurbations the rates of net out-migration are highest for the better off (Table 1).

Chart 4 Population movements

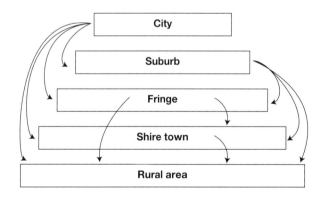

Source: Tony Champion, Presentation to DETR, 1999

Why do people move?

2.9　The evidence from some surveys is that people move mainly for accommodation and personal reasons but also because of job factors. Those who were looking for better areas appeared to identify these with suburban and rural areas. Other surveys and research have identified low crime rates, good health facilities and low cost of living as key factors. In assessing the importance of local services in decisions on moving, people cited schools most frequently (Table 2).

Table 2 Reasons for moving, all households resident for less than one year

Accommodation related reasons	21%
Personal reasons	27%
Better areas	9%
Job related	11%
Other	32%

Source: *Living in Urban England: Attitudes and Aspirations,* DETR, 2000

The consequences of the exodus

2.10　The exodus has four main consequences:

* continuing pressure for the expansion of towns and cities into greenfield development with a continuing legacy of underused land and buildings within urban areas;

* a wider social impact on rural communities with local people being priced out of the housing market by better-off people leaving the towns and cities and villages becoming dormitories;

* previously healthy communities near city centres experience increasing social polarisation, with those who cannot move living in a poor local environment with high levels of crime. In some areas this results in a very low demand for housing and the areas potentially face abandonment; and

* wasteful use of natural resources and increased pollution as those who move out travel greater distances to get to work, shops and the places where they spend their leisure time. A higher proportion of journeys also tends to be made by car rather than on foot or by public transport.

Poor quality of life and lack of opportunity

2.11　There are both significant differences between the major conurbations and the rest of the country on key quality of life indicators and between different neighbourhoods within the same town or city.

Differences between urban areas and the rest of the country

2.12 Generally, the major conurbations perform less well than the rest of the country on most key indicators.

2.13 The average performance of pupils of all ages in areas such as inner London the main metropolitan centres and some of the smaller cities is below that for the country as a whole. In most of the conurbations those in the central city perform less well than those in the outer areas (Chart 5).

Chart 5 Educational performance Examples of conurbations and central cities: 1998

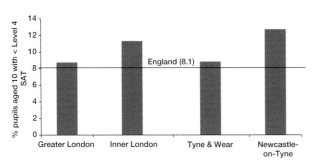

Source: The State of English Cities, DETR, 2000

2.14 City dwellers are both more likely to fall victim to crime and more likely to worry about it. For example, in 1999, 5% of adults in inner city areas experienced violence – nearly twice the rate in rural areas. 6.3% of inner city households were burgled compared with 2.6% of rural households.

2.15 There are also differences between areas on a number of key health indicators. People in urban areas are less likely to say that they have good health than those living in suburban and rural areas. Mortality ratios are higher in cities although for some diseases such as cardiovascular disease and longstanding illnesses there are no significant differences between urban, suburban and rural areas.

2.16 Most deprivation remains concentrated in the conurbations. Over 70% of those who live in one of the 10% most deprived wards live in one of the main conurbations, including London.

Differences within urban areas

2.17 Within towns and cities there have always been contrasts between the conditions for the rich and the poor. However, the gap between the poorest and the rest of society appears to have widened in the 1980s and become more concentrated in some areas.

2.18 In some areas the problems are very longstanding. In particular, many of the areas of East London identified by Charles Booth in the late 19th century still show up today as having the worst social deprivation. In three wards in Tower Hamlets over 80% of children live in households that depend on means tested benefits.

2.19 Even in those towns and cities with significant deprivation there remains a sharp local contrast between prosperous areas and those with most deprivation. For example, Sheffield has two wards amongst the least deprived in the country just across the city from some deeply deprived areas (Map 1). Conversely, in many of the more prosperous towns and cities there are pockets of deprivation.

Map 1 Deprivation in Sheffield

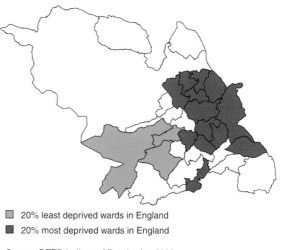

☐ 20% least deprived wards in England
■ 20% most deprived wards in England

Source: DETR Indices of Deprivation 2000

2.20 The deprived areas have been studied intensively in the preparation of the National Strategy for Neighbourhood Renewal. This is discussed further in Chapter 6.

Attitudes

2.21   As we noted in Chapter 1, we tend to be happy with our area wherever we live. However there are differences between those in the more central parts of cities and those in outer suburbs and rural areas, with those in central areas being significantly less satisfied (Table 3). Part of those differences reflect the characteristics of those areas and the importance of services to them. Public transport is seen as much better in core urban areas than in the suburbs; conversely education and general appearance are considered to be much better in the suburbs.

Table 3 Satisfaction with Local Area by Type of Area: 1998/99

	Percentages				
Area Type	Very Satisfied	Fairly Satisfied	Neither	Slightly Dissatisfied	Very Dissatisfied
Urban	35	40	8	9	7
Suburban/ Urban	42	40	5	9	5
Suburban	55	34	4	5	2
Suburban/ Rural	64	28	3	3	1
Rural	77	19	2	2	1

Source: Living in Urban England: Attitudes and Aspirations, DETR 2000

The impact of poor quality of life and opportunity

2.22   The extent to which our conurbations generally and deprived areas in particular lag behind the rest of the country is of concern for three reasons.

*   As a matter of social justice all should have the opportunity to share in the nation's growing prosperity and improving quality of life.

*   It is one of the factors that motivates people to move out of urban areas.

*   The denial of opportunity to those living in certain areas means that they are not able to contribute to our economic performance.

Economic performance

2.23   The overall structure of our economy has changed significantly in the last 50 years. Manufacturing has given way to services and there has been a relative decline in unskilled manufacturing jobs which were traditionally carried out by men. The main conurbations and cities were disproportionately affected by these changes (Chart 6). Some areas were very hard hit. Cities such as Birmingham lost up to a third of their manufacturing base in a period as short as five years. Single industry towns dependent on steel, shipbuilding or coal lost their economic heart. There has been a growth in service sector employment and particularly finance and business services (Chart 6). While smaller towns and rural areas have benefited the most, the growth in these sectors has gone some way to offset the decline in manufacturing in our cities and conurbations.

Chart 9 Per cent change in employment by sector 1981 - 1996

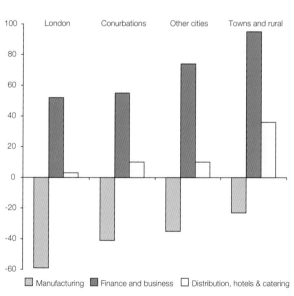

Source: ONS Annual Employment Survey in Turok I, Edge N: The Jobs Gap in Britain's Cities, 1999

2.24   The biggest increases in flexible forms of employment – including part time employment – have taken place outside the main cities (Chart 7).

Chart 7 Change in employment by sex and status (000s), 1981 - 1996

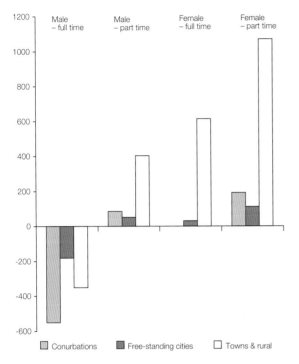

Source: Turok I, Edge N: The Jobs Gap in Britain's Cities, 1999

2.25 The contrasts between areas is well illustrated by Chart 8. Towns and rural areas have seen more or less continuing growth in employment over the last 20 years. The free standing cities have just about held their own but the conurbations are now beginning to see some recovery from the declines in the 1980s and early 1990s. In 1998/99 rates of employment were still lower in inner London, metropolitan areas and cities compared with other types of area.

Chart 8 Change in employment 1981-96 (1981 = 100)

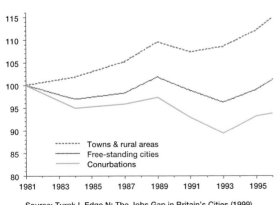

Source: Turok I, Edge N: The Jobs Gap in Britain's Cities (1999)

Why poor performance matters

2.26 The implications of the under-performance of certain urban areas are far wider than the prosperity of the immediate area:

- there is a clear link between poor economic performance and poor performance on key quality of life indicators: growing prosperity is an important driver in tackling deprivation;

- the impact on the wider region: the economic performance of an urban area affects the surrounding area – the main conurbations affect their entire region;

- the under-performance of the economy as a whole.

2.27 We cannot allow such poor performance to persist if we are to meet the challenges of the future. We can expect the nature of work to continue to change as new technologies and e-commerce have an increasing impact. There may be more part-time working and more self-employment. Companies will become more internationally mobile and will be looking at a wide range of factors in assessing the attractiveness of places to locate and do business.

The environmental impact of urban living

2.28 Unsurprisingly, as 80% of us live in urban areas, our towns and cities are responsible for a large proportion of the pollution and other adverse impacts on the environment:

- towns and cities create the vast majority of our domestic waste yet we currently re-cycle and compost only 9% compared with over 30% in many areas of Europe and the USA. The use of landfill to dispose of most of our waste has implications for the surrounding countryside;

- over 40% of vehicle mileage is in built-up areas;

- nearly half of all the UK's road transport emissions of airborn particles (a key air pollutant) arises in urban areas;

- while it has improved significantly in recent years, air quality is a significant issue in many urban areas. Often it is the poorest communities that suffer most;

- city-dwellers are more likely to be exposed to higher levels of noise; and

- people express considerable concern about their local environment identifying traffic congestion, fouling by dogs, litter and rubbish and traffic fumes as particular concerns.

2.29 We are beginning to understand better the impact the way we live in towns and cities has on the global environment. For example, Chart 9 suggests that there is a relationship between the density of urban areas and the consumption of petrol. If we are to secure sustainable development, we will need sustainable cities.

Chart 9 Relationship between urban density and fuel consumption

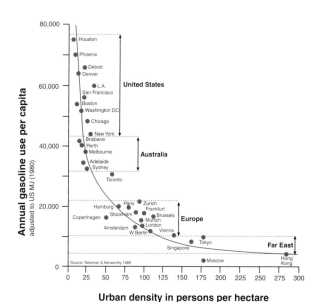

Source: Towards an Urban Renaissence DETR, 1999

Consequences of environmental impact of urban living

2.30 The Government has already set out a broad framework to promote sustainable development in *A Better Quality of Life (DETR, 1999)*. Clearly any strategy to reduce the adverse environmental impact of how we live today has to focus on urban areas both because they are the source of much of the problem and because the scope for measures such as increased re-cycling are so much greater. But how we plan for the future shape and design of our towns and cities can contribute more directly in minimising the use of green field land by re-using derelict and contaminated land.

How we develop can reduce car use, increase the use of public transport and have a positive impact on the local and global environment.

The positive signs

2.31 At the beginning of the chapter we set out the prospect that a continuation of current trends and behaviour could damage both town and country. If we accommodate the demand for homes through unplanned sprawl we will damage the countryside and undermine cities and towns, leading to a lower quality of life for everyone.

2.32 But there are more positive signs. By the mid 1990s many of the conurbations and some of the major cities were growing. In others the decline had slowed (Table 4). Greater London particularly has seen a significant increase in population in which natural growth and international migration have outweighed migration outwards to the rest of the UK.

Table 4 Average annual population change (%) of conurbations

Conurbations	Average annual population change (%)		
	1971-1981	1981-1991	1991-1997
Greater London	−1.01	−0.45	0.06
Greater Manchester	−0.49	−0.54	0.00
Merseyside	−0.87	−0.88	−0.04
South Yorkshire	−0.16	−0.37	0.00
Tyne & Wear	−0.56	−0.47	−0.01
West Midlands	−0.53	−0.51	0.00
West Yorkshire	−0.15	−0.23	0.02
Former county of Cleveland	−0.03	−0.38	−0.01

Source: The State of English Cities, DETR, 2000

2.33 There is more specific, although as yet limited, evidence of re-population of some parts of the urban cores. In Central Manchester it is estimated that the resident population has grown from 300 in 1998 to 6000 in 2000. These incomers are mainly single or couples without children. They are often in professional occupations and include students. Initially public financial support was needed to encourage the reuse of redundant buildings but there is now market led growth.

2.34 The cities and conurbations have seen a growth in total employment in the 1990s. In the main this comes from adapting more successfully to attract and retain a higher proportion of the growing sectors of the economy. Birmingham, Leeds and Manchester attracted jobs in private services including finance. (Table 5). Some of the common factors in those relatively more successful places include the role of the city as a regional centre and the strength of local higher education institutions. There is also a strong contribution from cultural activities and tourism. Some of the cities developing most strongly have begun to market themselves as "24 hour cities".

Table 5 Trends in sectoral employment in conurbations

	% change in employment in manufacturing & construction 1991-1996	% change in employment in private services 1991-1996	% change in employment in public services 1991-1996
Greater London	−15.3	9.6	−1.5
Greater Manchester	−10.4	6.7	7.2
Merseyside	−24.8	−3.2	−5.0
South Yorkshire	−4.7	1.3	0.8
Tyne and Wear	8.6	−5.5	5.1
West Midlands	−7.4	8.7	−2.4
West Yorkshire	−5.6	5.5	8.9
Former county of Cleveland	−12.1	7.3	−11.6

Source: The State of English Cities, DETR, 2000

2.35 These positive developments depend in part on the wider improvement in the economy. They are not yet shared by all the major cities. It is encouraging however that similar changes are seen in the United States. There the core cities are beginning to grow, although still less quickly than the suburbs, and unemployment is falling in the central cities.

A vision which meets the challenges

2.36 There is a clear alternative to continuing as we are. It builds on the existing strengths in every town and city; it builds on the example offered by our best towns and cities; it builds on the early signs of what will work in improving towns and cities; it means recognising the linkage between the five main issues we identify:

- **to accommodate the new homes we will need by 2021** through a strategy that uses the available land, including, in particular, brownfield land and existing buildings in urban areas wisely to create homes which people will find attractive and planning carefully any expansion of urban areas;

- **to encourage people to remain and move back into urban areas**, particularly the centres of our major cities and conurbations, by making them places which offer a good quality of life. This means having an attractive urban environment employment opportunities and good quality services;

- **to tackle the poor quality of life and lack of opportunity in certain urban areas** as a matter of social justice, to enable all to share in and contribute to our growing prosperity and to enhance the overall attractiveness of cities to people and business;

- **to strengthen the factors in all urban areas which will enhance their economic success** especially in those areas with a wider regional impact; and

- **to make sustainable urban living practical, affordable and attractive** to enable us to reduce the emissions, waste products and other local and global environmental impacts.

2.37 That comprehensive approach to the future of our towns and cities can be encapsulated in a simple vision which is at the heart of this White Paper.

2.38 This vision for towns and cities is part of the Government's overall strategy for tackling poverty and social exclusion and fostering economic growth in a way that benefits all citizens. Throughout this strategy there is a recognition that social, economic and environmental issues are interdependent – and that failure to act effectively in all of these areas leads to polarised cities that cannot succeed in the longer term.

2

A new vision of urban living

Our vision is of towns, cities and suburbs which offer a high quality of life and opportunity for all, not just the few. We want to see:

- **people shaping the future** of their community, supported by strong and truly representative local leaders;

- people living in **attractive, well kept towns and cities** which use space and buildings well;

- good design and planning which makes it practical to live in a **more environmentally sustainable** way, with less noise, pollution and traffic congestion;

- towns and cities able to **create and share prosperity**, investing to help all their citizens reach their full potential; and

- **good quality services** – health, education, housing, transport, finance, shopping, leisure and protection from crime – that meet the needs of people and businesses wherever they are.

This urban renaissance will benefit everyone, making towns and cities vibrant and successful, and protecting the countryside from development pressure.

Delivering better towns and cities

Contents

Our approach

3.1   To achieve our vision of towns and cities which offer a high quality of life and opportunity for all, we are:

- establishing a framework for **effective partnerships** to allow properly **joined-up strategies** to be developed and implemented with local people and all the organisations involved in tackling local problems;

- putting in place **effective policies and programmes** to provide the building blocks out of which local strategies can be developed; and

- providing the **rescources required to make a difference.**

3.2   Chapters 4 to 6 outline the comprehensive package of policies and programmes we have put in place over the last three years and the further action we are now proposing. This chapter briefly summarises the resources we have committed to make those polices and programmes effective. It then explains the principles that underlie our approach to making those policies and programmes work to the benefit of local communities.

Resources to make a difference

3.3   In this year's Spending Review the Government has provided substantial extra resources for all the services that contribute to a good quality of life. By 2003/04 an extra £33 billion a year will be made available. Most of this will be spent in urban areas (where 80% of the population live). Services provided in urban areas are, of course, also used by people living in rural areas.

Extra resources: Spending Review 2000

	baseline £ billion 2000/01	increase £ billion by 2003/04	average annual real % increase
Education	38.8	10.4	5.4
Health	45.3	13.7	6.1
Transport	4.9	4.2	20.0
Housing	3.0	1.6	12.0
Criminal justice	12.5	2.7	4.1
Leisure, culture, sport	1.0	0.2	4.3

Criminal Justice data: England and Wales
All other data: England

3.4 The impact of this extra money has yet to be felt: it starts to come on stream from next April. Service providers are currently planning how best to use the additional resources.

3.5 The extra money is additional to baseline funding totalling some £106 billion. As part of the new partnerships we are keen to develop, we are anxious to see both the baseline funding and the extra resources used where they can have the greatest effect.

3.6 The public funding is only part of the story. Private sector investment in our towns and cities has always outstripped public investment and will continue to do so. We need to work in closer partnership with the private sector to channel its energy and resources to the good of the community as a whole.

Targets for improved performance

3.7 The quality of public services depends not only on how much the Government spends but also on how effectively it spends it. In 1998 the Government set out in Public Service Agreements (PSAs) the service improvements, key reforms and much needed modernisation that we would deliver. These targets drive good performance by clarifying the outcomes on which services ought to focus and encouraging all to rise to the level of the best. They are also an important step in improving democracy, transparency and accountability as they illustate to the public exactly what the Government will deliver in return for taxpayers' investment. The key PSAs are included in Chapters 4-6 alongside the programmes and policies which are the building blocks for successful towns and cities.

3.8 In Spending Review 2000 we built on the success of the first PSAs by setting challenging targets for the next three years. We also set out for the first time 'floor targets' for education, employment, health, crime and social housing specifying the minimum standards to be delivered in all areas. These will have a key role in narrowing the gap between deprived areas and the rest of the country. They will require departments to allocate a generous proportion of the additional resources to deprived areas. They are set out in the shaded pages at the end of Chapter 6 (pages 114-128).

Delivering change in the local area

3.9 The right policies and programmes and the resources to implement them are essential if we are to bring about a lasting improvement in our towns and cities, but they are not sufficient. They must be applied so as to meet the needs of people wherever they live – in town or city centres, in suburbs or, indeed, in rural areas.

3.10 This means applying them in a way that recognises that:

- **no two people and no two places are the same.** As Chapters 1 and 2 show, our towns and cities vary tremendously. Most are thriving. Some face significant difficulties. All face different challenges and have different strengths and opportunities. There can be no 'one-size-fits-all' approach handed down from Whitehall. We need strategies that are tailor-made to suit each local area and which reflect the different needs of all communities including minority ethnic groups;

- **people have a right to determine their future and be involved in deciding how their town or city develops**. A clear message from the regeneration initiatives of the last 30 years is that real sustainable change will not be achieved unless local people are in the driving seat. It is not enough to consult people about decisions that will impact on their lives: they must be fully engaged in the process from the start; and

- **everybody must be included**. This is both a mark of a decent society and plain good sense. We have a rich diversity of different ethnic cultures in our towns and cities. We should value and foster this. We must be prepared to invest more in people to enable all to have the opportunity to share in and contribute to our national prosperity. If we fail in this we both demean the individual and waste a valuable resource. Allowing people to be excluded also risks alienation and disruptive and anti-social behaviour.

3.11 In short, we need local strategies developed with local people to meet the needs of local people. This requires effective partnerships between all those concerned at national, regional and local level. In particular, it requires effective local authorities: councils that listen to, lead and build up their local communities; councils that work in partnership with business, minority ethnic and faith communities, voluntary organisations and other service providers with the common objective of improving the quality of life of all in their area. To do this councils need to break free from old fashioned and inward looking practices and attitudes. Radical reform is required. That is why we embarked on a 10-year programme to modernise local government when we published our White Paper, *Modern Local Government, In Touch with the People*, in 1998.

Delivering our vision for towns and cities

- **People come first:** policies and programmes must be tailored to meet the different needs and aspirations of individual communities and include everyone.

- **People must shape their own future.** Led by modern councils, that are responsive and accountable to their local communities, local partnerships should develop a vision for their area and a strategy to deliver it within the framework set out in this White Paper.

- We are creating a framework for **effective partnerships** involving national and local government, regional bodies, business, service providers, and the full range of voluntary and community organisations.

- This will allow **policies and strategies at all levels to be joined-up** and encompass sustainable development of the urban environment, economic performance, social issues and services.

Effective and accountable local government

3.12 Local authorities have a key role as deliverers of essential local services and it is important that they do this well and in a way that meets the needs of local people. But their role needs to be much wider.

3.13 Local authorities need to engage local communities. Too often local people feel powerless to influence what happens in their community. They are daunted by, or alienated from, officialdom. They certainly do not see it as working on their behalf and interested in their views. We want to change this. We want local participation from all local communities, irrespective of their origins. Without real commitment from the community we will not be able to make the best use of the resources available.

3.14 Local authorities should:

- let people have a real say in the decisions which affect the day-to-day lives of their communities;

- provide strong local leadership developing, in partnership with others, a vision and strategy for the local area through Community Planning; and

- deliver quality local services that people want.

3.15 Our local government modernisation programme allows councils everywhere to modernise and reform so that they can fulfil these roles. We are putting in place a new legal framework which gives councils the opportunity to develop a new culture and new ways of working. We are giving councils:

- new duties to consult people on how they want to be governed locally and to bring forward proposals for a new constitution to enable more efficient, transparent and accountable decision making;

- new powers to promote the economic, social and environmental well-being of their local areas and a new duty to produce a Community Strategy;

- new duties to secure best value in service delivery; and

- better financing arrangements with real incentives to improve performance.

Local leadership

3.16 Strong local leadership is essential if there is to be effective action. Leaders must engage and earn the respect and confidence of all local communities. They should lead the debate locally about the development of the community. Once a strategy has been agreed, they should drive forward its implementation with their partners, setting clear goals and determining priorities.

3.17   So that councils can provide efficient, transparent and accountable local leadership the Local Government Act 2000 gives them new duties: first to consult their communities on how they want to be governed locally; and second, in the light of what local people say, to come forward with a new constitution. For major urban areas the constitution must take one of the following broad forms:

- a mayor directly elected by the people with a cabinet;

- a cabinet with a leader elected by the council; or

- a mayor directly elected by the people with a council manager appointed by the council.

3.18   In all cases the constitution must include effective and powerful ways to hold the mayor, leader, cabinet or council manager publicly to account.

3.19   International experience suggests that directly elected mayors are often the best option to provide the leadership which larger towns and cities need. In such places whenever councils consult their communities about how they want to be governed locally they should refer to this experience so that they give people a real choice. Where local people think that a directly elected mayor is right for their town or city we want such a mayor to be elected.

New powers

3.20   The Local Government Act 2000 also gives local authorities unambiguous powers to promote the economic, social and environmental well-being of their areas. There is now no doubt that local authorities can take the action required to deliver better towns and cities. Local authorities can now do what is necessary to boost their area unless it is specifically prohibited by legislation.

Best Value

3.21   The Local Government Act 1999 gives local authorities a duty of Best Value under which they are required to produce Best Value Performance Plans showing their record in delivering services and their plans for improving them. This promotes both greater efficiency and improved accountability. Authorities have to review the performance of all their services over a five year period. They must:

- **challenge** why and how a service is being provided;

- **compare** their performance with others;

- **consult** local taxpayers, service users and the wider business community; and

- use fair and open **competition** to procure services.

Better financing arrangements

3.22   We have begun consultations about new ways of financing local authorities with a view to finding a better system than the present one.

Local Public Service Agreements

3.23   We are also piloting local authority Public Service Agreements (PSAs). These are, in effect, contracts between central government and local authorities under which local authorities would agree challenging targets for improving the delivery of key services in return for greater operational freedom and financial rewards. We aim to reach agreement with local authorities on 20 pilots for 2001/02 ahead of a wider roll out in 2002/03.

Local Strategic Partnerships

3.24   No one knows a place better than the people who live and work there. They must be at the heart of the process to develop a strategy that will work in their area. That is why Local Strategic Partnerships are the key to our strategy to deliver better towns and cities.

3.25   Local Strategic Partnerships (LSPs) will bring together the local authority, all service providers (such as schools, the police and health and social services), local businesses, the full range of community groups and the voluntary sector. They will:

- develop a Community Strategy to cover the local authority area. This should look at all aspects that contribute to quality of life together; identify strengths and weaknesses; and set out a long-term vision that has been agreed with all the key stakeholders;

- agree priorities for action and monitor local performance against agreed local indicators taking into account national and regional targets; and

- co-ordinate the work of more local or more specific partnerships dealing with particular neighbourhoods or issues.

3.26   Local Strategic Partnerships will not be just another partnership on top of the many already in place at the local level. They should look to rationalise and co-ordinate the existing partnerships.

3.27 Community Strategies are needed not just to identify and tackle failing areas: we also need to build on success. No community is guaranteed continuing prosperity. All areas need to take positive action to take control of their future in a changing world rather than just waiting to react to events. This is particularly important in towns and cities that are regionally significant as their influence stretches well beyond local boundaries. Local Strategic Partnerships are also responsible for developing neighbourhood renewal strategies in areas in which deprivation is a significant factor.

3.28 Local Strategic Partnerships should take a fully joined-up approach that brings together economic, social and environmental issues. They will not be starting from scratch. In some areas effective strategic partnerships already exist and have produced comprehensive strategies. In most areas a great deal of very valuable work has already been done on many important elements of the strategy. For example, Local Agenda 21 groups have been developing strategies to put the principles of sustainable development into practice at the local level and are on target to produce their strategies by the end of the year. This work can be built on to produce Community Strategies.

New Commitment to Regeneration

The "New Commitment to Regeneration" approach developed by the Local Government Association provides models of how a Local Strategic Partnership (LSP) can work. 22 local authority-led strategic partnerships have been set up to:

- agree comprehensive long-term visions for their area;

- produce strategic action plans;

- agree individual partners' responsibilities in delivering the action plan;

- look at opportunities to focus public programmes to meet local priorities; and

- monitor progress against locally developed performance indicators.

Such partnerships can be tailored to local circumstances to produce a better overall result. Sandwell and Croydon, for example, both have different, but successful partnerships.

The **Sandwell Civic Partnership** prepares a Community Strategy with four thematic partnerships at its core, covering learning, health, economic development and urban form.

Benefits include:

- the development of an e-learning environment with 700 access points;

- a youth strategy developed by young people;

- the creation of a prototype healthy living centre; and

- plans for a major centre for community arts and technology as a catalyst for regeneration.

The **Croydon Partnership** seeks to secure long–term prosperity and has achieved notable success by involving a range of local businesses.

Benefits include:

- a marketing company, Croydon Marketing & Development, sponsored by the 28 town centre businesses and the council;

- an 'ambassadors' scheme to promote Croydon to business; and

- specialist working groups to strengthen small businesses, secure inward investment and raise awareness about social exclusion.

3.29 The Government does not intend to specify the geographical area which such partnerships should cover or the tier of local government at which they should be established. These are matters for local agreement, depending on local circumstances and the need to build on successful existing partnerships.

Working together at all levels

3.30 A Community Strategy will not be fully successful if it is developed in a vacuum. What happens at the local level depends to a significant extent on what is happening elsewhere in the region and nationally – and vice versa. In particular, the conurbations and major cities have an impact that stretches well beyond their administrative boundaries and influences the entire region. Policies and programmes need to reflect this. To get the best possible result we need to recognise the different roles which different places play and co-ordinate action at the neighbourhood, local, regional and national levels so that we all pull together rather than against one another.

Neighbourhood action

3.31 The problems faced by the most deprived areas and communities demand more specific action targeted at the neighbourhood level. Following extensive consultation, the Government's Social Exclusion Unit is currently drawing up an action plan that will set out how the National Strategy for Neighbourhood Renewal will be implemented. The aim is to narrow the gap between the most deprived areas and the rest of the country. The measures it will contain need to be seen within the strategic context set out in this White Paper, as action at the neighbourhood level will only be fully successful if it is co-ordinated with the steps being taken in the wider local area and at the regional and national level.

Regional action

3.32 Government Offices for the Regions (GOs) will have a new and enhanced responsibility for joining-up regional Government activity. They will work closely with the business-led Regional Development Agencies, which will have a key role in driving forward economic and physical change. Together with Regional Chambers, Regional Planning Bodies and the Regional Cultural Consortia, they will provide the strategic context for towns and cities.

National action

3.33 The Government will both support and lead. Through this White Paper we are setting out the broad framework. We have also provided substantially increased resources through the Spending Review.

3.34 We also recognise the need to co-ordinate better both between departments and between the centre, the regions and the local level. To do this we have established stronger co-ordination arrangements both within central government and between central government and local authorities.

An inclusive society

3.35 We want all who live in urban areas to have the opportunity to achieve their full potential – regardless of irrelevant factors such as race, age, gender, faith or disability. We also want all to have their say in policy development and implementation, and to have equal access to services, as set out in the Government's Equality Statement of 30 November 1999.

Disabled people

3.36 The Government believes that disabled people should have the same opportunities as everyone else to participate as equal citizens in our towns and cities. We:

- have set up the new Disability Rights Commission, whose goal is a society where all disabled people can participate fully as equal citizens, enforcing comprehensive civil rights for disabled people;

- are implementing a new Code of Practice on rights of access for disabled people, so that from October 2004 businesses and other service providers will need to ensure that their services are accessible to disabled people by improving access to their premises where reasonable;

- are introducing regulations under the Disability Discrimination Act to ensure that in future new land-based public transport vehicles are accessible to disabled people;

- are ensuring that the needs of disabled people are taken properly into account in policies to reduce car dependency, recognising that for many severely disabled people the car will remain the most viable choice;

- are reviewing the disabled persons parking scheme – the blue (formerly orange) badge scheme – to ensure that the scheme continues to serve those with the greatest need; and

- will provide some form of exemption for disabled people from congestion charging and workplace parking levy schemes where these are introduced.

Women

3.37 Women are often the backbone of local community life – they make a huge contribution to improving the quality of life for their families and the wider community as mothers, volunteers, residents and workers.

3.38 The Government is working to widen opportunities for women, improve maternity rights, raise child benefit, extend childcare and introduce universal changes such as the minimum wage to ensure that all women can make genuine choices themselves.

3.39 Women are still paid less than men. The Government has introduced initiatives to tackle the problem of this pay gap including the National Minimum Wage, the new 10p tax rate and the new Part–Time Workers Regulations. The Government has also made a commitment to promote family-friendly initiatives, including through the *Fairness at Work* White Paper.

3.40 It is important that services respond to the needs of women. For example, childcare is a vital support for women and families, enabling them to take up opportunities – the Sure Start programme and the National Childcare Strategy will make a big difference. Women also make considerable use of services such as public transport. We are working with transport operators to ensure that their services respond to the needs of all customers including women. And it can be particularly hard for women living in areas plagued by crime – our Crime Reduction programme is funding innovative, practical projects to build on best practice and to develop techniques to prevent crimes such as domestic violence, rape and sexual assault.

Ethnic minorities

3.41 Black and minority ethnic communities are more likely to live in urban areas creating a richly diverse culture. Current employment rates are lower for ethnic minorities, and particularly for ethnic minority women than for the ethnic majority, though employment rates in some ethnic minority groups have risen in the last 15 years at a similar rate to the ethnic majority.

Sandwell Bangladeshi Women's Association

Local Bangladeshi women in Sandwell have taken the lead in identifying their needs and in seeking new ways to help fulfil their potential. Working in partnership with others, they have:

- set up a skills centre, to train and develop the skills of local Bangladeshi women;

- taken a key role in managing the local Muslim centre; and

- set up the ASHA Project, which provides bi-lingual training, advice and support in volunteering and health care. ASHA, the Urdu word for hope, symbolises the work of the project.

Through this work, the women have learnt how to take a full role in their community.

3.42 The Stephen Lawrence Inquiry report highlighted the inequalities that exist in the services provided by some of our public institutions to ethnic minorities. Although the report focused on the police, the report drew attention to what is a wider problem.

3.43 The Race Relations (Amendment) Bill before Parliament as this White Paper went to print will implement a key recommendation of the Inquiry. It will outlaw discrimination not only by the police but by all public authorities (with limited and justifiable exceptions). It will also make it a duty of specified public authorities to work towards the elimination of unlawful racial discrimination and to promote equality of opportunity and good relations between people of different racial groups. This general duty will be supported by specific duties, which can be enforced if necessary by the Commission for Racial Equality. These duties will be underpinned by statutory codes of practice to provide practical guidance to public authorities.

3.44 We are also tackling this issue through other administrative action including the programme outlined in the Home Office report *Race Equality in Public Services*. This document brings together the key issues for minority ethnic communities and sets out how the Government is using performance management to ensure that race equality is at the heart of Government thinking. This approach is consistent with our view that the public sector must lead by example on race equality.

Faith communities

3.45   The significant overlap between ethnic and faith groups in many cases means that the engagement of faith communities as stakeholders in renewal can be vital. Moreover faith communities can command valuable resources and social capital in terms of networks, buildings, voluntary activity and leadership skills. These can be especially important in deprived areas if other forms of institutional support have been eroded.

3.46   Faith communities are a distincitve part of the voluntary and community sector. To realise their potential contribution to renewal and social inclusion is a challenging agenda both for faith communites and for other stakeholders.

3.47   The Government is comitted to the involvement of faith communites and supports the Inner Cities Religious Council in DETR. This multi-faith Council acts as a forum for consultation across government departments with a particular focus on regeneration and the drive for inclusion.

Young and old

3.48   We want to ensure that older people have access to high quality services and opportunities to participate in society, so that they are able to live secure, fulfilling and active lives. We also want to encourage involvement by older people in deciding priorities, helping shape policies and ensuring they have more say and control over services they use.

3.49   The Inter-Ministerial Group for Older People (IMG) has helped ensure that older people's issues are at the centre of our thinking on policy development and service delivery. The Secretary of State for Social Security leads the IMG and also been appointed as Cabinet Champion for older people to drive the work forward. The 'Better Government for Older People' programme has developed and tested strategies to deliver local services in new and innovative ways in 28 pilot areas across the UK, promoting better co-ordination and responsiveness to older people.

3.50   A variety of current and planned actions and policies will help improve the opportunities and choices for older people in urban areas. For example we are:

- helping people over the age of 50 find employment through a £270m New Deal programme launched in April 2000, providing job seekers with tax-free financial support, a personal adviser and a training grant to help with updating skills;

- conducting a nationwide take-up campaign to make pensioners aware they could be claiming under the Minimum Income Guarantee;

- promoting opportunities for volunteering and raising awareness of the positive contribution older people can make to their community through volunteering;

- promoting a culture of life-long learning, including giving older people a voice on the new Learning and Skills Council;

- improving leisure opportunities for older people, including through increased funding to enable all our major national museums and galleries to offer free access to everyone over 50 from this year;

- providing grants under the Home Energy Efficiency Scheme to help pensioners insulate and warm their homes. By 2004 the scheme is expected to have helped 800,000 households, around 60% of which will be pensioner households; and

- helping improve transport options, including through guaranteeing that from April 2001 all pensioners will pay no more than half fare on their local bus.

3.51   We need to ensure that the welfare of young people is safeguarded. We have undertaken a *Cross-Departmental Review of Young People at Risk*. Its purpose was to identify cost-effective policies for helping young people to make the transition safely and successfully from childhood to adulthood.

3.52   Two new initiatives to be introduced as a result of this review are:

- the Connexions Service to help all 13 to 19 year olds make the most of their educational, vocational and development opportunities, and to prepare for successful transition to adulthood and the world of work. The Service will be delivered via a range of means, including a network of personal advisers who will give advice and guidance, broker access to specialised support and, in some cases, provide personal development opportunities; and

- a Children's Fund, established to tackle child poverty and social exclusion. The Fund will be worth a total of £450m over three years.

3.53 We are, in particular, concerned that young people should not face unsafe and insecure housing situations. Action includes:

- the establishment of the Rough Sleepers Unit which has set in place a strategic approach to tackle rough sleeping and to address its root causes;

- a new Safer Communities Supported Housing Fund to provide new housing and support for young people at risk and other vulnerable people;

- the Youth Homelessness Action Partnership to address the problems of youth homelessness;

- an objective that by 2003 all under-18 teenage lone parents who cannot live with family or a partner should be placed in supervised semi-independent housing with support; and

- an amendment in April to the *Code of Guidance for Local Authorities on the Allocation of Accommodation and Homelessness* to indicate that we generally expect local authorities to regard careleavers and other homeless 16 and 17 year olds as "vulnerable," and hence in priority need for accommodation.

A challenge to deliver

3.54 This White Paper is about making all urban areas successful places for all people. This chapter has described the arrangements we have established to enable all concerned – communities, local and regional bodies, business, voluntary groups and central government – to work together. The rest of the White Paper summarises the policies and programmes we have put in place. These provide the building blocks needed to construct action plans to tackle the interrelated economic, social and environmental issues which affect people's quality of life whether they live in towns, cities or suburbs. The challenge to all concerned is to take those building blocks and make them work in each community for the benefit of all.

3

Places for people

The Government's aim is to create high quality towns and cities which people can be proud to live in. They must be attractive, clean, safe and well cared-for, combining vitality and interest with practicality, sensitivity to the environment and continuity with the past. They must be well designed and planned, and make the best use of previously-developed land and existing buildings.

Contents

Introduction

The urban environment

4.1 Where we live affects how we live.

4.2 The urban environment can be harsh and intimidating or it can encourage people to feel at ease. It can be impersonal and make contact between people difficult or it can foster a sense of community. Towns and cities can be laid out so that people have little choice but to use their cars for most journeys – and as a result they can exclude those who do not have the use of a car – or they can be designed so that walking, cycling and public transport are the natural and attractive options.

4.3 We want our towns, cities and suburbs to be places for people – places that are designed, built and maintained on the principle that people come first. They should contribute to the quality of life and encourage healthy and sustainable lifestyles. They should be places in which we want to live, work, bring up our children, and spend our leisure time. They should be places which promote economic success and allow people to share in rising prosperity, attracting and retaining successful businesses.

4.4 In England we have long had a tradition of creating towns and cities of quality and beauty – places that can bind communities together. Many of our best towns and cities retain that quality or are recreating it today. But in other places it is a tradition we have lost.

4.5 We need to recapture this tradition. In most places this means making the most of our existing urban fabric, maintaining it well and making incremental improvements. In some places nothing short of a complete physical transformation will do. Where we have the opportunity of new development we must ensure that it is of the highest quality.

The Urban Task Force

4.6   In 1998, we commissioned the Urban Task Force under Lord Rogers to look at the causes of decline in English towns and cities and to recommend practical solutions to bring people back into urban neighbourhoods. Its report set out convincingly how good planning, design and management can help bring run down, neglected places back to life.

> *We need a vision that will drive the urban renaissance. We believe that cities should be well designed, be more compact and connected ... allowing people to live, work and enjoy themselves at close quarters within a sustainable urban environment which is well integrated with public transport and adaptable to change*
>
> Lord Rogers of Riverside

4.7   We whole-heartedly support the vision set out by the Urban Task Force. We agree with most of its recommendations and have already implemented many of them. Where we have not accepted a recommendation it is because we believe that there is a better way of achieving the underlying objective, not because we disagree with the objective. The Annex summarises our response to the Urban Task Force.

4.8   This chapter looks in turn at three aspects of making urban areas places for people:

- **better planning and design.** We will use the planning system and other tools to promote better quality and improve the design of urban areas;

- **bringing previously-developed land and empty property back into beneficial economic or social use**, so that they contribute to, rather than detract from, the urban fabric; and

- encouraging local authorities and others to **look after the existing urban environment better** and work to improve it further.

4.9   A key component of each of these is working with and influencing the private sector, whose combined investment in urban areas will always be far greater than that of the public sector.

4.10   One direct way of doing this is through fiscal measures and other incentives. These play an important part in each of the following sections. They include:

- National fiscal incentives. As announced in the November 2000 Pre-Budget Report the Government plans to introduce in Budget 2001:

    - an exemption from stamp duty for all property transactions in disadvantaged communities (page 63, paragraph 12);

    - accelerated payable tax credits for cleaning up contaminated land (page 60, paragraph 7);

    - 100 per cent capital allowances for creating 'flats over shops' for letting (page 56, paragraph 3);

    - package of VAT reforms to encourage additional conversion of properties for residential use (page 56, paragraph 3).

- Consultation on a range of Local Government Finance Measures:

    - rate relief for Small Businesses (page 88, paragraph 5);

    - options for funding Town Improvement Schemes (page 70, paragraph 5);

    - a Local Tax Re-investment Programme (page 63, paragraph 12).

- A range of other measures still under development or discussion:

    - review of planning obligations including the option of introducing impact fees (page 48, paragraph 6);

    - potential tax relief for Urban Regeneration Companies (page 63, paragraph 7);

    - possible reduction of VAT for listed buildings that are places of worship (subject to discussion with the European Commission) (page 72, paragraph 5);

    - consultation on a possible Community Investment Tax Credit (page 97, paragraph 7).

4.11   Many of these instruments and many of the other measures outlined in this and other chapters need to be used selectively to target specific regeneration and urban renaissance issues in priority areas. They have been developed with that in mind, providing a toolkit of measures which can be used by local partnerships to address particular needs in particular places.

Better planning and design

4.12   Where there is a need or opportunity for new development in towns and cities we must ensure that it is of the highest quality. In particular we must ensure that it:

- makes the best use of the land we have available; and

- is built in a sustainable way that is sensitive to the needs of people and the impact urban living has on the environment.

Using space well

4.13   The UK is one of the most densely populated countries in the world. Over the last 30 years our population has grown by three million. As well as there being more of us, more of us are living alone and living longer. As a result, in the period between 1996 and 2021 we may need to accommodate up to 3.8 million additional households.

4.14   70% of these additional households will be single person households. But although the size of households is decreasing, this is not always reflected in the variety of homes being provided to meet the needs of the future.

4.15   We also build at very low densities and, in the past, have squandered land. Recent housing development in England has been built at an average of 25 dwellings per hectare. That compares unfavourably with the 35-40 dwellings per hectare of many of our older suburbs – made up of semi-detached and terraced houses with gardens – and with current development densities in many other countries.

4.16   We have also been allowing too many new houses to be built on greenfield sites. This threatens the countryside and fuels the flow of people away from urban centres towards the edge of towns and cities and beyond.

4.17   This is unacceptable. We have therefore set a national target that, by 2008, 60% of new housing should be built on brownfield land or be provided by the conversion of existing buildings. We have also abandoned the old predict and provide approach to housing need and introduced a new policy of Plan, Monitor and Manage to guide future housing provision at the regional and local levels. This allows a more flexible approach which recognises that circumstances change and is not driven by rigid targets based on household projections alone.

Sustainable development

4.18   Past planning policies have also allowed:

- major new shopping developments outside urban areas which have threatened the competitiveness and viability of town and city centres, as well as neighbourhood shopping;

- the fragmentation of communities and separation of the places where people shop, work and spend their leisure time from the places in which they live;

- patterns of development which encourage unnecessary travel, damaging the environment and undermining sustainable development; and

- poor quality design and layouts and poor building practices which in turn create poor quality places.

4.19   We cannot continue like this. We need design and planning policies that promote a better quality environment and encourage inclusive communities.

The way forward

4.20   We need an approach to the design and development of urban areas which:

- makes efficient use of the available land and buildings and reduces the demand for greenfield development;

- provides homes which are attractive and environmentally friendly;

- encourages well laid out urban areas with good quality buildings, well designed streets, and good quality public open spaces;

- allows people to get to work easily and to the services they need like local shops, post offices, schools and health and leisure facilities; and

- makes good public transport viable and makes walking and cycling attractive options.

4.21   This does not mean cramming people closer and closer together. It means development at reasonable densities which protect open spaces and respect the need for privacy. We know from experience in this country and abroad that, with good design, it is possible to create places which fulfil all these ambitions and which people want to live in.

Popular new residential development at Chatham Maritime
built at a density of 40 dwellings per hectare
(Picture courtesy of Countryside Properties)

Modernising Planning

4.22   Sound planning policies and an efficient,
inclusive planning system are essential to the delivery of
better towns and cities. Our wide-ranging Modernising
Planning programme will make far-reaching changes at
the national, regional and local levels.

4.23   At the national level, we have issued new
Planning Policy Guidance (PPGs) to support urban
renaissance.

4.24   In particular, our new guidance on housing
(PPG3) is central to our drive for an urban renaissance
and its effective implementation by all local authorities
is vital. It:

- aims to provide an adequate supply of housing;

- gives priority to development of brownfield sites
  before greenfield land. Our national brownfield target
  is 60% by 2008 and we are asking each region to
  set targets in Regional Planning Guidance and
  Development Plans to contribute towards achieving it;

- explains that planned urban extensions are likely to
  be the next most sustainable option after building
  within urban areas;

- seeks to ensure more efficient use of land;

- promotes greater housing choice and affordable
  housing;

- promotes mixed development, so homes are closer
  to jobs and services;

- promotes conversion and re-use of empty buildings;
  and

- promotes higher quality development and more
  imaginative design and layout.

How the planning system turns policies into better developments

- **National planning policy** is set out in 25
  Planning Policy Guidance notes covering topics
  such as housing, transport and town centres.

- **Regional planning guidance** sets out the
  strategic planning policies for each region. It
  is prepared by Regional Planning Bodies in
  consultation with other stakeholders. Each
  Regional Plan is approved by the Secretary
  of State for the Environment, Transport and
  the Regions, subject to any amendments
  that may be needed to make it consistent
  with national policies.

- Local authorities prepare **development
  plans** to provide the local context for
  individual planning decisions. Local authorities
  must take into account national and regional
  planning guidance in preparing these plans
  and in deciding individual planning applications.
  The Government can intervene in a
  development plan or "call-in" an individual
  planning application if it raises issues of
  more than local importance, including
  compliance with national or regional guidance.

PPG3 represents a step change in the way we plan for
housing following our earlier White Paper *Planning for
Communities of the Future* (February 1998). We want to
see local councils and housebuilders implementing the
new policy now – not when all the greenfield allocations
made under a previous policy have been exhausted. We
are therefore supporting delivery by:

- a new **Greenfield Housing Direction** (October
  2000) which gives teeth to our new approach. We
  want local authorities to plan to provide sufficient
  housing but give priority to redevelopment of urban
  brownfield sites first. The Direction means that major
  greenfield developments are not given planning
  permission without the Secretary of State first being
  given an opportunity to consider whether they are in
  line with PPG3;

- the new **National Land Use Database** which provides a clear picture of how much brownfield land is available for development across England, and where it is; and

- **good practice guidance**. We, and others, have already published advice on good design (e.g *By Design* and *The Urban Design Compendium*) and monitoring (*Monitoring Provision of Housing through the Planning System*). We will publish further practical guidance on urban housing capacity studies and managing land release to help local authorities on the ground.

These new planning policies need to be disseminated and embedded in the planning system. We will be working with local authorities and other key partners to ensure that this happens.

4.25 We are also strengthening planning policies on:

- **town centres** – between 1979 and 1997, 13 million square metres of out of town shopping floor space was developed. This undermined the viability of many town centres and encouraged increased use of car travel. We have now strengthened guidance (PPG6) that new retail and leisure developments should not be permitted on out-of-centre sites if there is an option of developing closer to the town or city centre; and

- **transport** – forthcoming guidance (PPG13) will propose better integration of transport and planning policies so that jobs, services and other facilities will be more accessible by public transport, cycling and walking. We want planners to be more proactive so that, wherever possible, the need to travel will be reduced.

4.26 To complete the picture we now intend to **revise PPG1 – General Policy and Principles** – to reflect our vision for better towns and cities and for protecting the countryside. The new guidance will explain how we should plan for sustainable communities, promoting economic success along with social inclusion and protection of the environment. It will, as envisaged in the Urban Task Force report, ensure that planning policies fully support the drive for an urban renaissance.

Sustainable urban extensions

The Prince's Foundation and English Partnerships supported by DETR and the Council for the Protection of Rural England (CPRE) are undertaking a series of projects under the heading **Planned Through Design** to help demonstrate how the social, economic and environmental sustainability of new housing developments can be improved.

Planned Through Design has:

- tested, through case studies in Northampton and Basildon, a new approach to planning urban extensions where key players work together to design better places;

- shown how the policies in PPG3 for design, density and community development will produce more sustainable places than has previously been the case; and

- underlined the importance of developing innovative ways to involve local people in planning.

a

b

Plans for an urban extension in Basildon:
a) is the conventional developers' product showing what a volume housebuilder would be expected to build.
b) shows the alternative where intensified development would produce a housing yield of 1,120 homes with seven hectares of parkland and open space.
(Images courtesy of The Prince's Foundation)

4.27 At regional level, we have introduced new arrangements for Regional Planning and published up-to-date guidance (PPG11). We now expect regional players to prepare Regional Planning Guidance (RPG) instead of such guidance being prepared centrally; we have introduced stronger links with transport and the needs of business; and we have ensured that the new arrangements are more inclusive by involving key stakeholders. The new approach is up and running with public examinations held and independent panel reports published in 6 regions to date.

Other action

4.28 We are also:

- Taking action to improve **local participation and the delivery of the planning system** at the local level;

- setting a good example and **showing the benefits of good design** through the design of public buildings and practical demonstrations;

- improving the **skills of planners, designers and developers**; and

- improving the **quality of construction**.

The action in these areas is described in the following pages.

The new Gateshead Millennium Bridge is designed by civil engineers Gifford and Partners and Wilkinson Eyre Architects and will be ready by Spring 2000.
The bridge will create a mile-lone circular riverside promenade, and will join-up the two riverside cycleways on the north and south banks of the Tyne.
It will link the newly-revived Newcastle Quayside with new developments at Gateshead Quays on the south bank of the Tyne. These include the Baltic Centre for Contemporary Art in the former Baltic Flour Mills building, the Music Centre Gateshead and a leisure complex with luxury hotels, café-bars and resturants.
Photograph: David Lawson. Courtesy of Gateshead Council.

The Stephen Lawrence Trust

In the summer of 1998 Doreen and Neville Lawrence formed a charitable Trust in their son's name to create opportunities for black and disadvantaged young people to develop in the field of architecture. The Trust aims to provide a richer mix of architects, bringing a class and cultural diversity to those who will shape tomorrow's built environment for all of us.

So far the Trust has developed bursary programmes for young people in the North of England in collaboration with Sheffield University, in London with the Architectural Association and overseas with the Caribbean School of Architecture in Jamaica. It is now hoping to extend its programmes into Africa and to develop bursaries with the University of South Africa.

In order to provide a lasting tribute to Stephen, the Trust is also developing an Educational and Arts building in Deptford, South East London, called the Stephen Lawrence Technocentre. This will provide training for students, particularly black and disadvantaged young people, interested in pursuing further education in architecture and other related design and environmental studies.

BETTER PLANNING AND DESIGN
1: Modernising planning: improving local participation and delivery

1.   Many people care deeply about their local area and would welcome greater opportunity to be involved and influence how it is designed and planned. Local participation can help shape development proposals and encourage community buy-in. At the same time, business and the public want a planning system which promotes competitiveness and is efficient and responsive; where development plans do not take years to be put in place; and where planning applications and appeals are dealt with quickly.

Delivery

2.   The Government wants to see better delivery of local planning services. Through our Modernising Planning programme we have taken action on:

- **planning concordats**. We have agreed a planning concordat with local government which sets out our joint expectations for an effective and efficient planning service. The Local Government Association has published a Planning Users Concordat agreed with business and the voluntary sector to underpin this through local action;

- **development plans**. We have published new national policy guidance (PPG12) and introduced revised statutory arrangements to improve the speed, quality and delivery of Local and Unitary Development Plans;

- **planning applications**. Some 500,000 planning applications are made each year. To provide the housing, jobs, recreation and other facilities which towns and cities need, decision-making needs to be efficient. We are using the Best Value regime to raise performance; and we are considering setting statutory performance standards to drive up the performance of the worst authorities;

- **planning appeals**. We introduced new statutory appeals procedures in August 2000 to speed up the handling of the 13,000 or so decisions that are appealed each year. We have set the Planning Inspectorate demanding targets for decision-making and we expect those involved in appeals to play their part;

- **electronic planning**. A £3m Capital Modernisation Fund project is enabling the Planning Inspectorate to develop a Planning Internet Portal. This will provide an electronic appeals handling service between the public and the Inspectorate, as well as giving access to a wide range of guidance and advice; and

- **major projects**. We have consulted on proposals to improve the way major infrastructure projects are handled.

Local participation

3.   Our new national guidance on Development Plans (PPG12) presses for plans to be shorter and clearer, less clouded with detail, and make more use of criteria-based policies which can respond flexibly to change. We make clear the role that Supplementary Planning Guidance can play at a more local level. However, we want to go further to help local communities give expression to their views on how their area should be developed. To do this we will:

- further encourage the preparation, in close consultation with local communities, of development briefs, design guides and master plans (see page 50) setting out how planning policies can be applied in local areas. We will set out further advice in national guidance on the role that these can play as Supplementary Planning Guidance, to be taken into account in making planning decisions on individual development proposals; and

continued

4

- investigate alternative approaches to local plan making. This will include considering the value of more strategic spatial plans at local authority level and of 'neighbourhood' plans. We intend to review the effectiveness of neighbourhood approaches where they have already been tried, the scope for such plans to be used as Supplementary Planning Guidance and the need for wider reform.

4.   One additional way of involving local communities in the planning and design process is through the development of architecture and design centres. These can provide a venue for exhibitions, public discussion and displays of planning applications and development proposals. There are already twelve such centres around the country funded by a variety of bodies including the Commission for Architecture & the Built Environment (CABE), Regional Development Agencies, Local Authorities and the Arts Council.

5.   The Government is keen to see more of these centres develop and will continue to work with CABE, the RDAs and others including the Regional Cultural Consortia to consider how this process can best be supported. CABE has a particularly important role to play in coordinating the efforts of the centres and developing best practice, although it is important that they should continue to be set up at the local level by local partners so that they can encourage real community involvement.

Planning obligations

6.   We also want to see further improvements in the operation of the planning system. We therefore intend to issue a consultation paper shortly on planning obligations. These are arrangements by which contributions from developers can be used to offset the negative consequences of development or to secure positive benefits that will make development more sustainable. This could include, for example, new infrastructure associated with the development, or money to help pay for local environmental improvements.

7.   We believe that the current planning obligation system should be reviewed to ensure that the public fully understands how it works and how obligations are negotiated between local authorities and developers. We intend to retain the broad principle that contributions should be made by developers to meet local needs and we will ensure that the system offers a fair deal to both developers and the community. Options which will be considered include widening the range of local improvements which can be supported by planning obligations and introducing impact fees which might reflect more of the cost of development in terms of its environmental consequences.

1. We want good planning and design in new development and renovation to be second nature for everyone, in both the public and private sectors. To achieve this we need to demonstrate the benefits of good practice through real life examples and encourage people to take the importance of good design and planning more seriously.

Public buildings

2. In the past public buildings like railway stations, schools and libraries were often the pride of towns and cities, setting high standards of design. More recently, with some notable exceptions, the public sector has been associated with poor design and quality. We want to re-establish the tradition of good design in public buildings, making it the rule rather than the exception.

3. To do this we have:

- established a Ministerial champion for good design in each Government Department;

- given the Commission for Architecture & the Built Environment and English Heritage a key role in working with the public sector and others to promote quality in building contracts.

Wider role for the Commission for Architecture & the Built Environment

4. CABE has the task of campaigning for, and advising the Government on quality design both in public buildings and the wider built environment. It has already advised on more than 40 development schemes and has had a major impact on the profile of design issues. At present it is sponsored by the Secretary of State for Culture, Media and Sport. In view of its relevance to the responsibilities of DETR it will in future be jointly sponsored by the two departments. This will add to its authority and give it a more strategic role.

5. It is essential that CABE focuses on the quality of the built environment as a whole. We expect the Commission to promote the highest standards of urban design and to use its enabling and review roles to help develop skills and best practice in both the public and private sectors.

Examples of good design

6. Real, practical examples of good design are invaluable in encouraging higher standards. This is what the Prince of Wales has done with his scheme at Poundbury. It is also an important part of the Government's Millennium Communities Programme which is designed to show how we can build sustainable, environmentally responsible communities for the 21st Century.

7. The first millennium community, on the Greenwich Peninsula, is now under construction and people will be moving in by the end of this year. It is being built using construction techniques which will create at least 50% less construction waste and will lead to a development which uses 80% less energy and 30% less water than its conventional equivalent. It will also provide:

- attractive, mixed-tenure, higher density housing making optimum use of open space and providing 20% affordable housing, well-integrated into the rest of the development;

- mixed-use development, with good employment, retail, education and health facilities, and innovative design creating a safe environment; and

- good public transport links reducing car dependency and with an emphasis on cycling and walking within the village.

Artist's impression of Greenwich Millennium Village
(Photograph courtesy of Greenwich Millennium Village Limited)

continued

8. A second millennium community, at Allerton Bywater, a former coalfield community in West Yorkshire, is now taking shape. And we are hoping to initiate a further five communities over the coming 12 to 18 months. We would like each of these to be in a different type of location with different characteristics, including a seaside town, but all must share the key features of sustainable urban communities developed in Greenwich and Allerton Bywater. The third community will be in the Cardroom Estate, East Manchester. As with the existing communities, proposals for the development of the site will be the subject of an open competition and judged against a comprehensive brief agreed with the community.

Master planning

9. Master plans are about setting out a vision for an area undergoing change and a strategy for implementing that vision. They are about taking the initiative in terms of design, layout, houses, jobs and services in order to build or strengthen communities. Critically, they must show local people what an area might look like in the future. All master plans should involve local communities in their development.

10. Master plans can be given formal status in the planning system by being adopted as Supplementary Planning Guidance. We want to encourage this. In keeping with the views of the Urban Task Force, the Government will lead by encouraging all significant area regeneration projects to use master plans and all regeneration partnerships to work within their agreed framework.

Master planning – A vision for the future

Birmingham has drawn up a master plan for the regeneration of the east side of the city centre. This follows the successful regeneration of Birmingham Westside at Brindleyplace. The aim of the Eastside master plan is to transform a tired industrial zone into a high quality development of residential, office, commercial and leisure facilities. The master plan includes:

- an £800m regeneration of the Bull Ring. The new Bull Ring will include new stores, cafes, restaurants and leisure facilities;

- the creation of a nine acre City Park, which will be designed in consultation with the local community;

- the replacement of the elevated section of the Queensway Inner Ring Road and the Masshouse area of car parks and isolated businesses with a major urban boulevard;

- a new Learning Centre; and

- a new educational, science and technology centre at Millennium Point.

(Images courtesy of Birmingham City Council)

BETTER PLANNING AND DESIGN
3: Improving the skills of planners, designers and developers

1. Achieving good planning and design depends critically on the ability and skills of the professionals involved. There are many in both the public and private sectors with good skills in individual disciplines, but we have a shortage of people with high quality cross-disciplinary urban design skills. We have already:

- brought the design professions together to promote a new multi-disciplinary approach to training in design and urban development to be driven forward by CABE;

- challenged the development professions and employers working with the higher education system to include more education in design in their approved syllabuses; and

- initiated research on the provision of training for urban design.

2. But the Government agrees with the Urban Task Force that additional activity to improve skills, particularly in the regions, is needed. As a result it intends to:

- Promote **Centres of Excellence** by asking regional and local partners including local authorities, higher education institutes, existing architecture and design centres and centres for the built environment, and professional bodies to work with the Regional Development Agencies to determine the best approach to improving skills and training in each region.

  A North West Centre of Excellence in regeneration and urban renaissance skills is shortly to be established. Regional partners, working with the North West Regional Development Agency, the Centre for Sustainable Urban and Regional Futures at the University of Salford, and the Centre for the Understanding of the Built Environment, have developed firm plans for a centre to encourage the exchange and dissemination of best practice in regeneration. Initially it will offer web-based information and links to existing centres of expertise on all aspects of urban regeneration – physical, social and economic. It will aim to provide an integrated approach to regeneration disciplines in a flexible format available to members of local regeneration partnerships as well as regeneration professionals. The centre will be closely linked with other national and regional bodies such as the proposed Centre for Neighbourhood Renewal and CABE. Other regions will be able to make use of the centre and draw on its experience in considering arrangements for improving skills in their own regions.

  In London it is also planned to set up a Regional Resource Centre to provide a variety of short courses and on-line education. The Centre, supported by the London Development Agency, will involve academics from relevant universities and other educational establishments, the professional institutes and potential users.

  CABE will play a mentoring and evaluation role in the development of skills and training at the regional level and will report back on progress to the new Cabinet Committee on Urban Affairs (see Chapter 7, page 130, paragraph 7.10).

- Consider a **new urban design theme** for a future Beacon Council round to promote better professional skills within local authorities by giving national recognition to local authorities able to demonstrate excellence. Current Beacon Council themes already give local authorities the opportunity to compete to become a Beacon for quality town centres.

- Initiate an **exchange of international experience** by undertaking three high profile secondments: to DETR itself as part of the advisory team following up this White Paper; to a national body such as CABE to consider the differences in skills and training that exist between ourselves and other countries and how international experience could help; and to a regional or local project such as one of the new Urban Regeneration Companies.
  This will provide an immediate start on a wider programme of secondments envisaged by the Urban Task Force.

4

BETTER PLANNING AND DESIGN
4: Quality construction and building regulations

1. Improved planning and design needs to be complemented by improvements to the quality of construction. Following the report by Sir John Egan's Task Force, *Rethinking Construction*, we have established the Movement for Innovation and the Housing Forum, to encourage improvements in the construction and house-building sectors, and the Central and Local Government Task Forces to promote change among public sector clients. The aim of these bodies is to bring about radical improvements in:

- the quality and sustainability of construction and design;

- the speed and reliability of project times and budgets;

- the lifetime costs of buildings; and

- respect for the community and the environment.

2. They do this by using real projects, across the country, to show the benefits of:

- more client focused, innovative procurement methods;

- streamlined building processes and better measurement of performance;

- a team approach to design and construction; and

- making the most of standardised components and off-site construction.

3. Through this approach these projects are showing that good design can result in both efficient construction and benefits for the environment and the community. They are also showing that designs can reflect local distinctiveness as well as using latest technologies, and that there are commercial benefits for companies in approaching design and construction in teams and partnerships.

Movement for Innovation (M4I)

M4I demonstration projects have:

- shown profits of 8% in 1999, compared to 4.7% in the industry as a whole;

- been completed on time 68% of the time as opposed to 62% of the time; and

- been completed on budget 62% of the time as opposed to 45% of the time.

They have also demonstrated effectively the advantage of modern, sustainable build practices. The primary school below in Great Notley, Essex combines sustainable design with low cost and natural materials to bring the whole-life cost of the building down. A continuing process of review between designers and the construction team maintained quality and efficiency, and consultation with the local community ensured that the building would serve the broader needs of the area.

Primary School in Great Notley, Essex.
(Photograph: Tim Soar, Courtesy of Essex County Council/ Design Council)

continued

4. We have also taken action to make construction more environmentally sustainable. *Building a Better Quality of Life* sets out best practice on this showing how we can reduce consumption of materials and land, minimise waste, re-use recycled materials, promote energy efficiency and manage site operations better to avoid pollution. *Building a Better Quality of Life* was prepared in close consultation with the industry and its clients.

Next steps

5. Following a successful start our priority now is to disseminate the principles behind Rethinking Construction and the Movement for Innovation even more broadly in the regions and down the construction supply chain. We will be doing this through:

- a programme of regional road-shows to promote best practice among public sector clients;

- using the Construction Best Practice Programme's regional network and the Rethinking Construction clusters to promote improved practices and spread awareness especially in small and medium sized enterprises and occasional clients; and

- developing new centres of construction innovation with the industry's trade and professional institutions, construction research organisations and the universities.

6. We will also continue to press construction clients to drive forward improvements in performance. For our part we have committed all government departments and agencies with significant construction programmes to targets for best practice procurement and sustainability across their building procurement by March 2002.

7. In response to a challenge from the Deputy Prime Minister, the Construction Clients' Confederation is developing the Clients' Charter which will be launched in December this year. Clients in the public and private sector who sign up to the charter will commit to Rethinking Construction; to measure their own performance and that of their suppliers; to drive up standards on their construction projects and to develop new ways of working with the industry. After its launch we will encourage local authorities and others to adopt the charter and demonstrate the potential for improved building practices.

Building regulations

8. Building regulations play a key part in assuring the safety and quality of the urban environment, addressing issues like structural safety, fire safety and noise proofing.

9. We are currently modernising the way building regulations work and updating their requirements in a number of important ways. For example:

- we have extended building regulations on access and facilities for disabled people to new housing;

- we have consulted on improved energy efficiency standards, to take account of the contribution they can make to tackling climate change, and will be announcing changes to the regulations next year;

- we are reviewing standards of sound insulation between houses and looking at extending the regulation to cover external noise. We will be consulting on proposals shortly; and

- we are looking at whether building regulations could be used to improve security standards in new homes.

4

Bringing brownfield sites and empty property back into use

4.29 In England today, 58,000 hectares of brownfield land (equivalent to an area the size of the West Midlands conurbation) is either vacant, derelict or available for redevelopment, and more becomes available every year. Over 700,000 homes are also empty. Most of these are empty because they are in the process of being sold, let or repaired, but around 225,000 have been vacant for at least a year. There is also a substantial amount of empty or under-used commercial property with potential for conversion to mixed-uses including housing. In a country like ours, this is an enormous waste of a very precious resource.

4.30 Most of these areas of land and most empty properties are in urban areas – in the centre of towns and cities, in edge-of-town sites and also in our suburbs.

4.31 Where they exist they can detract from the quality of the rest of the urban environment, they dent confidence in the future of the area and in some cases they can be a hazard to health.

Challenges and opportunities

4.32 Unused brownfield land and empty properties arise for a number of reasons:

- as a natural side effect of a dynamic society and economy. These properties and areas of land come and go and will often be redeveloped and reoccupied quickly depending on the condition of the local economy;

- as a legacy of our industrial past. As many industries have disappeared, scaled down, or moved to edge-of-town or greenfield sites, we have been left with large areas of land which can be difficult to redevelop and, in some cases, are contaminated; and

- as a result of the decline of an area and a decrease in its popularity. This is often a particular problem for residential areas.

4.33 Where brownfield land and empty properties are not redeveloped or reoccupied quickly they become, not only a wasted resource, but a problem for the whole community. We need to recognise their value and do what we can to make them easier to recycle, particularly, in the case of empty buildings, where they represent part of our country's heritage. If we are successful they offer a major opportunity to redevelop and revitalise towns and cities, building on existing character and diversity.

The way forward

4.34 To grasp this opportunity we need to make our brownfield land and empty properties fit for new purposes, clean them up where they are contaminated and turn them back into community assets whether it be as homes or as a new area of open recreational space.

4.35 Action to do this needs to recognise the different circumstances of different places and the reasons they are underused. It could involve:

- encouraging businesses to move back into small brownfield plots or vacant buildings in a town centre;

- bringing about the wholescale transformation of an area by rehabilitating old industrial land, developing new uses and building new communities; or

- bringing new services to a residential area to improve its popularity.

Coalfields regeneration

In 1998 the Government announced a long-term action programme to help communities suffering acute physical dereliction and deprivation as a result of the pit closures of the 80s and 90s.

This was backed by an investment package of £354m over three years which included:

- **the Coalfields Regeneration Trust** – set up in September 1999 with more than £50m of Government investment to support a range of community initiatives providing new work and training opportunities and support for community enterprise;

- **the Coalfields Enterprise Fund** – being developed to bring together public and private sector investment to support small firms with high growth potential in coalfield areas; and

- **Network Space** – a joint venture between English Partnerships and the Langtree Group plc to build and manage workspace premises in up to 20 coalfield locations to meet the needs of new and expanding small businesses.

In addition **English Partnerships and the Regional Development Agencies** run a £380m coalfield programme to create lasting social and community benefits through the physical regeneration of vacant and derelict land and related social and economic projects. It is hoped that this programme will produce: 46,500 job opportunities; 17.5 million square feet of new industrial floorspace; almost 5,000 new houses; and more than 2,000 hectares of reclaimed land.

4.36 In the following sections we set out the action we and others are taking to:

- get **empty property** back into use and tackle low demand housing areas;

- identify brownfield sites and **assemble large areas of brownfield land** for redevelopment;

- reclaim **contaminated land**;

- encourage **investment and the return of enterprise** to brownfield areas; and

- give **regeneration agencies** like the Regional Development Agencies and English Partnerships the tools they need to bring about change.

The sundial in Victoria Park, Kingston upon Hull. The park was part of the transformation of the redundant Victoria Docks undertaken by a partnership involving the City Council and the private sector. It provides homes and facilities for a new community close to the city centre.
(Photograph courtesy of Kingston upon Hull City Council)

BRINGING BROWNFIELD SITES AND EMPTY PROPERTY BACK INTO USE
1: Tackling empty property and low demand housing

Empty property

1. Re-using existing buildings is important not only to revitalising declining urban areas but also to sustainable development. They are usually supported by existing infrastructure and, overall, their re-use is likely to be a more energy efficient and resource friendly than building new properties.

2. Local authorities and others are already doing a lot to bring empty properties back into use, particularly in areas of general low demand (see below). But we are now also:

- encouraging them to develop comprehensive empty property strategies;

- requiring them to report on their success annually; and

- working with the property professionals and the Housing and Property National Training Organisations to improve skills in this area.

3. In addition, following the recent announcement in the November 2000 Pre-Budget Report, we plan to introduce new fiscal incentives to encourage the use of empty or under-used properties:

- a **100% capital allowance for creating "flats over shops"** for letting. This will encourage better use of vacant and under-utilised space above shops and other commercial premises, helping to bring more life into commercial districts; and

- **Reform of VAT** to encourage additional conversion of properties for residential use. We will cut the VAT rate to 5% for residential conversions and remove the VAT burden on the sale of renovated houses that have been empty for ten years or more.

4. These measures will help encourage the redevelopment and better use of buildings, helping to reduce pressure for greenfield development as well as improving the urban environment for local residents.

5. Following the recommendations made recently by the Empty Property Advisory Group, we will also be:

- commissioning a guide for property owners and developers on residential conversion;

Smithfield Buildings, Manchester

The old Affleck and Brown department store in the northern quarter of central Manchester was suffering decline until English Partnerships stepped in with grant assistance to kick-start a revival.

Developers Urban Splash commissioned Stephenson Bell to restore the building as 80 loft apartments grouped round the original central atrium, now transformed into a spectacular winter garden. On the ground floor are shops, restaurants and workspace for one of the original tenants, with a basement gym and an upper level link to secure parking in an existing multi-story car park across the road.

Smithfield Buildings is now an eagerly sought-after address, supporting a thriving residential and commercial community. It is a textbook example of the contribution that an imaginative developer employing high quality designers can make to the revival of an inner city area. It won a DETR Housing Design Award in 1998.

(Photograph: Phil Sayer, courtesy of Pollard Thomas and Edwards)

continued

- commissioning a guide for local authorities on bringing property back into use;

- requiring government departments and other public sector landlords to report annually on their performance in bringing empty property back into use;

- asking the RDAs to address the issue of empty properties and to promote the action required to bring more of them back into productive use as part of the economic regeneration of urban areas;

- funding a series of regional seminars to raise awareness and spread best practice; and

- supporting a forum for local authority Empty Property Officers in each English region.

Tackling low demand housing areas

6. Low demand for housing in particular areas is a growing problem in many towns and cities – around 470,000 homes in the social rented sector and 375,000 in the private sector are in low demand or unpopular neighbourhoods. One consequence of this is the problem of negative equity for many home owners.

7. The causes are complex, and need a comprehensive response. In October 1999, an expert team made 40 recommendations for dealing with the problem. The Government has already acted on nearly every one.

8. A key finding was the need for stronger links between planning, housing and economic policy at regional, sub-regional and local level – to avoid problems of over-supply, and to prevent new greenfield developments competing with older, less popular housing. PPG3 (see page 44, paragraph 4.24) has been revised to change the way authorities assess housing supply so that it now includes buildings available for conversion. This means empty homes need to be considered as part of the potential supply before greenfield sites are considered.

9. The Housing Green Paper published in April also sets out a range of proposals for tackling low demand including:

- giving local authorities increased flexibility in managing their stock;

- encouraging more mixed communities;

- providing tools for local authorities to tackle low demand in the private sector such as making it easier for them to identify areas of particularly poor housing for Area Renewal; and

- reform of the lettings system and the power to grant assured shorthold tenancies and charge market rents on local authority housing.

10. The Good Practice Guide to local authorities on tackling low demand takes forward a whole series of recommendations on identifying low demand, management responses and more radical solutions such as selective demolition. It offers practical advice on a range of interventions in both the public and private sectors.

11. All of the actions set out above on both empty properties and unpopular housing will play an important role in shaping the future of an area and will need to be taken account of by the Local Strategic Partnership in their work on the area's Community Strategy (see Chapter 33, paragraph 3.15).

The Oakhill Estate in Rotherham. Built in the 1970s on a slum clearance site to the east of the town, the estate had long experienced social and environmental problems. These are now being addressed, in part through a programme of refurbishment and redevelopment.
(Photograph: Richard Townshend)

4

BRINGING BROWNFIELD SITES AND EMPTY PROPERTY BACK INTO USE
2: Land assembly

1. If we want to make the best use of previously developed sites in towns and cities we need to draw investment and businesses back into these areas. The first priority is to help developers find the right sites.

- **The national land use database** (see below) has been created to provide a picture of the extent and location of brownfield land available for development across England.

- Information about individual sites is also being made available to private companies through English Partnerships' internet-based **Strategic Sites Database**. It is planned to develop this service further.

National Land Use Database (NLUD)

The new National Land Use Database has been developed by DETR, Ordnance Survey, English Partnerships (EP), the local government Improvement and Development Agency (IDeA) and local authorities to provide a picture of the extent and location of brownfield land available for development across England.

The first survey carried out for the database in 1998 showed that 58,000 hectares of brownfield land was unused or potentially available for development in England at that time. A further survey will take place in 2001 and the database will be updated annually thereafter.

Information about individual sites has been disseminated via a website on a trial basis and it is planned to develop this service further. Research is also being undertaken to see how the database could be extended to other land uses. This will show the distribution of land uses in both urban and rural areas.

---

2. But information alone is often not enough. Urban sites are often fragmented and their ownership complex. Most land assembly is taken forward by the private and public sectors by agreement. However, in some cases the only option is to resort to the compulsory purchase powers of local authorities and also the RDAs.

Compulsory purchase orders

3. The compulsory purchase system enables land, and rights over land, to be compulsorily acquired in the public interest. The owners of property affected have a right to object and to be compensated if the CPO is confirmed. Following widespread criticism of the way the system operates we have undertaken a comprehensive review. We want to ensure that it operates speedily and effectively, whilst also being fair to those whose property is being acquired. The report of our Advisory Group of outside experts was published in July 2000. It concluded that new legislation was needed to clarify and modernise CPO powers, procedures and compensation provisions. We have just completed public consultations on the Advisory Group's recommendations and will publish a full response shortly.

4. In the meantime, there is no reason why local authorities, the RDAs and other partners should not get on and assemble suitable sites to facilitate development and promote regeneration in urban areas. We therefore intend to:

- issue revised guidance to local authorities drawing attention to the scope to use existing powers under the Town and Country Planning Act 1990 in support of major regeneration schemes. Leicester and Medway City Councils have demonstrated this can be done: there is no reason why other Councils cannot do the same;

continued

58

- issue guidance to the RDAs on the use of their CPO powers;

- encourage, where necessary, local authorities and their public sector partners, to use their land acquisition powers to help implement area regeneration strategies, for example, those being developed by the Urban Regeneration Companies; and

- tackle the "skills deficit". Some authorities have lost the know how and expertise in recent years to undertake compulsory purchase. We have therefore commissioned the production, for the first time, of a comprehensive manual and good practice guide. This will enable acquiring authorities to manage the process of compulsory purchase more efficiently and effectively, and with proper consideration for those whose property is being acquired. The manual will be published shortly.

5. We will also:

- bring forward proposals for legislation, when parliamentary time allows, to simplify, consolidate and codify the law on compulsory purchase, speed up procedures and make the compensation arrangements simpler and more equitable. This will address the powers needed by local authorities to undertake regeneration.

BRINGING BROWNFIELD SITES AND EMPTY PROPERTY BACK INTO USE
3: Dealing with contamination

1. Estimates of the amount of contaminated land in England vary considerably depending on the definitions used. In its report the Urban Task Force quoted estimates ranging from an area the size of Manchester to one bigger than Greater London (between 50,000 and 200,000 hectares).

2. Much of this land is only contaminated at a low level and is still in use. Relatively little of it is available for redevelopment but where this is the case it is usually possible to deal with the contamination quickly and easily. For more serious contamination, land treatment techniques are improving all the time and research and development is leading to innovation and better methods of risk assessment.

Assessment and regulation

3. The Government has recently introduced a new contaminated land regime to deal with sites where contamination is a problem for the current land use. The regime clarifies when regulators will intervene, what remediation will be required and who should pay. As a result it gives developers and owners more confidence about what they are taking on and that the requirements to deal with the contamination will be reasonable and proportionate. The regime is enforced by local authorities and, in some cases, the Environment Agency. Local authorities have a duty to inspect their areas to identify land where contamination is causing significant harm, or presents a significant risk of such harm, and ensure that proper remediation is carried out.

4. In most cases contamination is only an issue when a new use is proposed for the land. This is dealt with through the planning system when development is taking place. In these cases development plans set out local policies for dealing with contaminated land, including planning conditions to require proper remediation, which take account of national planning guidance on contamination. Following the introduction of the new contaminated land regime, we shall be updating our national planning guidance. A draft will be issued for consultation shortly.

Increasing Confidence

5. A key objective when dealing with contaminated land is to increase the confidence of those thinking of investing so that they are reassured enough to proceed. What investors need is greater certainty about the work which is required or reassurance that the necessary action has been taken. The new **Standard Land Condition Record** (LCR), being launched shortly by a consortium of key players in the contaminated land industry, is an important step forward in this. The LCR will record, for a given area of land, information about the physical and chemical nature of any contamination and about remediation. It can also include other useful information, for example information from a regulatory body or contractual information. It will be used by all the key players involved in its development with the intention that it will become an established document in the management and sale of contaminated land. The Government welcomes this development.

6. To ensure the reliability of LCR, the people filling it in will need to be suitably qualified. A system of personnel accreditation is therefore required and a working group is now working on this.

7. In additional the Government plans to increase investors confidence in projects involving contaminated land by accelerating the **tax relief** for cleaning it up.

8. The new tax relief will give investors immediate tax relief for their clean-up costs instead of having to wait until the land is sold. This will make projects to regenerate derelict sites more viable, help address the legacy of the past and reduce the pressure on greenfield sites.

continued

Encouraging new technologies

9. CLAIRE (Contaminated Land: Applications in Real Environments) is an initiative set up in March 1999 as a public-private partnership to encourage the use of innovative and practical solutions to deal with contaminated sites. It involves English Partnerships, the Environment Agency and the Soil and Groundwater Technology Association, and is supported by a wide range of private sector organisations.

10. CLAIRE operates by organising research and technology demonstration projects on contaminated sites using different remediation technologies and disseminating the results. It will also develop a research strategy to address the practical problems of contaminated land in the UK.

11. The network of CLAIRE demonstration sites will include examples of the range of industrially contaminated sites like coalfields, railway lands, manufactured gas plants, petro-chemical facilities and solvent sites. Its first demonstration project involved a thermal process to remove contamination on a petro-chemical site.

Reclamation of Royal Arsenal, Woolwich

In 1997, English Partnerships London (now the London Development Agency) undertook to develop and implement a regeneration strategy for the Royal Arsenal in Woolwich – a heavily contaminated site with a history of over 300 years of arms development and manufacture.

The project aims to create a mixed-use development with 700 homes, a light industrial scheme, a commercial/leisure centre and refurbished listed buildings for the Royal Artillary Museum and Greenwich Heritage Centre.

As part of the site investigation English Partnerships looked at alternative strategies to the traditional 'dig and dump' method common to this type of project. They discovered that the nature of the soil contamination meant they could minimise waste using innovative soil washing technology.

By October 2000, English Partnership had treated about half of the site and had washed and blended close to 125,000 cubic metres of soil – enough to cover twenty football pitches to the depth of a foot. This saved over 33,000 lorry movements and reduced considerably the need for landfill and quarry products to replace the soil.

The first stage of development, the heritage zone, will be completed around mid-2001.

BRINGING BROWNFIELD SITES AND EMPTY PROPERTY BACK INTO USE
4: Investment and enterprise

1. In the past, private sector investors have often steered clear of inner city and city fringe regeneration projects because they were seen as too risky with low rewards. If we are going to revitalise rundown brownfield areas successfully we have to change this perception and put in place measures to create the conditions for greater private sector involvement.

2. English Partnerships and the Royal Bank of Scotland have already set up a joint initiative, Priority Sites Ltd, which aims to develop industrial space where the private sector alone is unwilling to invest. During 1999/2000 Priority Sites Ltd estimates that it completed 22,000 square metres of business space providing accomodation for some 720 jobs. They are now working with the RDAs to identify further sites for development.

3. This is a good start, but we want to do more to encourage investment in brownfield urban areas.

Urban Regeneration Companies

4. One of the key recommendations of the Urban Task Force was to create Urban Regeneration Companies (URCs) which would work with a range of private and public sector partners, including the Local Strategic Partnerships, (see Chapter 3, page 33, paragraph 3.24) to redevelop and bring investment back to the worst areas in our cities and towns. Following the report we have supported the setting up of three pilot URCs – Liverpool Vision, New East Manchester and Sheffield One – which are developing a clear vision and strategy for key areas of these cities.

Liverpool Vision

Liverpool Vision, the country's first Urban Regeneration Company, is charged with the comprehensive physical transformation of Liverpool's city centre. Established by English Partnerships, the North West Development Agency, Liverpool City Council and the private sector, the company aims to create sustainable economic growth and new jobs by stimulating long term investment.

The company has assessed the major barriers to investment in Liverpool city centre to lie in the area's image, the quality of property, its environmental quality, and its transport and infrastructure. The partnership has produced a Strategic Regeneration Framework which will deal with these issues and allow the city to respond to changing circumstances in the future. It is supported by a range of initiatives including a bid for the title of European Capital of Culture, action to improve the public realm, development of city centre business opportunities and action to engage the people of Liverpool, and the region as a whole, in the city's development.

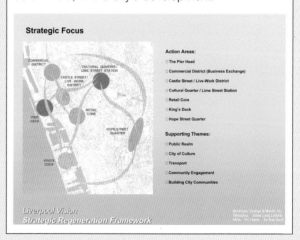

continued

5. The process of establishing the three pilot companies is being monitored and evaluated by the Government. So far this demonstrates that they have:

- been able to exert considerable influence by gaining the backing and commitment of their key partners;

- been responsive to the needs of the key partners including the community;

- been effective at putting together good major city strategies requiring considerable input of management and staff resources up-front; and

- resulted in better management of regeneration activities by avoiding a competing or uncoordinated approach to initiatives.

6. These preliminary results have convinced us that URCs are an effective means of undertaking major regeneration projects. We are therefore introducing a rolling programme of around 12 new companies over the next three years, with a limited number in each region. We will shortly be issuing new criteria for the principles guiding their operation and discussing proposals for new URCs with the RDAs and their partners which will be judged against these criteria.

7. As announced in the November 2000 Pre-Budget Report, the Government will continue to monitor the progress of URCs and will consider how a tax relief could help to promote their development.

English cities fund

8. We are also supporting the development of new ways to attract long term private investment in regeneration. English Partnerships and its private sector partners (AMEC and Legal and General) have been working on proposals for a pilot English Cities Fund, initially of £100m, to be invested in mixed-use developments in priority areas identified by the RDAs and their partners. The fund will be structured to expand rapidly to £250m (without further public sector capital) as private sector partners come on board.

9. If funds like the English Cities Fund can establish a track record in investment and returns other investment vehicles should follow. An example of such a vehicle is being developed by Morley Fund Management, the investment arm of CGNU. Their proposed Igloo Regeneration Partnership would look to fund investment in property development associated with regeneration projects, similar to those being considered by the English Cities Fund.

10. Typical projects would be mixed-use (residential and commercial) developments and are likely to be located in areas that have suffered economic and social change such as former manufacturing areas in edge-of-city locations. The Fund will be financed by private sector money and will undertake projects with a minimum value of £15m.

11. Currently proposals for the English Cities Fund are being considered in the context of the European rules on State Aids (see page 65, paragraph 6). Discussions with the European Commission are ongoing and an announcement will be made as soon as possible.

New Financial Incentives

12. In addition to these new initiatives the Government has announced that it intends to put in place a number of new measures which will encourage businesses and people to return to urban brownfield sites.

- We will introduce, in Budget 2001, a complete **exemption from stamp duty** for all property transactions in Britain's most disadvantaged communities. This will bring benefits to households and enterprises in these areas and will encourage the refurbishment and return to use of existing properties as well as new development;

continued

- We are currently consulting, in *Modernising Local Government Finance: A Green Paper*, on proposals for a new Local Tax Reinvestment Programme (LTRP). This would allow certain local authorities to keep any additional non-domestic rates and council tax they are able to collect from a defined area and for a limited period, and to plough that money back into projects and services which will benefit that area. This will not affect the amount of tax people pay – just the way the local tax revenue is distributed amongst local authorities. It will encourage local authorities to put in place the conditions which will make their area more attractive to businesses and residents. As new/expanded businesses or new residents come into the area the amount of resources available for reinvestment will increase.

- As set out on page 56, we also plan to introduce tax relief for residential conversions including a reduced VAT rate for residential conversions, an adjustment to the zero rate to provide relief for the sale of renovated houses that have been empty for ten years or more, and a tax relief for converting space over shops into flats for letting.

The award winning £25m redevelopment of Nottingham's Castle Wharf. The scheme has transformed a previously inaccessible and run-down area into one of the most vibrant parts of the city – attracting thousands of visitors and creating more than a thousand jobs.
(Photograph: British Waterways Photo Library)

1. The lead agencies for the physical regeneration of urban areas are the Regional Development Agencies (RDAs) and English Partnerships working in partnership with local authorities and others. The eight RDAs and the London Development Agency deliver the Government's physical and economic regeneration programmes in the English Regions. English Partnerships delivers national and cross-regional initiatives, supporting the RDAs' Regional Strategies.

2. The Government wants to see the activities of both the RDAs and English Partnerhships focused to address two different challenges. The first is about achieving *sustainable economic and social renewal* in declining areas to reclaim land, restore economic activity and improve services. The second is about providing for *sustainable economic growth* in areas which are expanding but which may have problems such as land shortages.

3. The RDAs and EP need to tackle both issues. To do this they need to build partnerships with the private sector, local authorities, Regional Chambers and others. Guidance is being developed for the regeneration agencies and their partners on developing effective area-based regeneration strategies, which will include a framework for monitoring and evaluating progress.

4. In keeping with the better focusing of RDA regeneration activities, the Government is also providing a major increase in resources for the agencies (see page 88, paragraph 5.25). This amounts to an increase of £500m by 2003/04 bringing funding for spending programmes up to £1.7 billion.

5. The Government is also giving RDAs much more flexibility on how they spend their resources in a newly combined single programme budget from DETR, DfEE and DTI starting on April 2002. Next year we will be taking a major step towards this single budget by increasing the RDAs' freedom to spend where they consider they can have the greatest impact in delivering national and regional policies. (see page 88, paragraph 5.26 for more details).

State Aids

6. The new resources which have been made available to the RDAs and the refocusing of their activities are, in part, a response to the decision, made last December by the European Commission, that the Partnership Investment Programme (PIP) operated by English Partnerships breached State Aid rules. These mean that aid given by a member state, in whatever form, should not distort competition, threaten to do so or favour certain companies in a way that might affect trade between member states.

7. PIP financed regeneration projects through a gap-funding mechanism where the public sector covered the difference between a developer's costs and his returns to make regeneration projects viable. This partnership approach benefited both sides, enabling regeneration activitiy which would not be carried out by the private sector alone, and in a more efficient way – through the better allocation of risk – than might be achieved by direct public sector intervention. The programme has now been closed down for new projects although transitional arrangements apply to those already being appraised.

8. Discussions are continuing with the Commission to find long term alternatives to PIP, particularly for engaging the private sector in regeneration. We hope to be working towards a positive outcome in the coming months. In the meantime the additional resources available to the RDAs will go a long way to allowing the pace of physical regeneration carried out by these agencies to be maintained.

Looking after the urban environment better

> *More than 90% of our urban fabric will still be with us in 30 years time....If we want to make the most of our urban assets, sustain the results of new investment and promote public confidence we must manage our urban environment carefully.*
>
> Urban Task Force Report

4.37 The first two sections of this chapter have looked at how to improve the quality of development in towns and cities and how to combat the waste of underused land and buildings. Those are vitally important but they only deal with a small proportion of the urban environment. We must maintain and improve the rest of the urban environment if towns and cities are to be attractive places in which people want to live and work.

Challenges and opportunities

4.38 Urban areas have a poorer local environment than non-urban areas with more litter, graffiti, noise and pollution. Although personal reasons such as finding a new job or a change in life style are often paramount, this can be an added incentive for people to move out. It can also be important in business decisions about where to locate and, therefore, have an impact on competitiveness and prosperity.

The importance of the local environment

Access to green spaces reduces stress and promotes well-being. Parks and open spaces are among the most valued features of the places people live.

Crime, vandalism, litter, noise and traffic are the most commonly reported problems in urban areas. These have an impact on the quality of urban life. For people about to move, crime and vandalism ranked alongside quality of housing and jobs as an issue where improvement could persuade them to stay.

The survey *Streets as Living Space* showed that people are more inclined to use their town and local centres if the urban environment is well cared for and pedestrian friendly.

4.39 The reasons for the poor quality of many urban environments are complicated. More intensive use of the environment in high density areas means that extra management is often needed. But the ability of local authorities to provide the necessary level of service has suffered a prolonged decline over many years due to:

- long-term central Government priorities which have focused their attention on areas like health, community care and education. This is undoubtedly right and will continue to be the case. but as a result some discretionary services like management of the urban environment have been squeezed; and

- a gradual loss of urban management skills and the ability to take a strategic, joined-up approach to maintaining the quality of the urban environment.

4.40 We need to take action to combat this decline.

Everyone's responsibility

4.41 We want to see an improvement in the quality of the urban environment for everyone, in all areas of towns and cities, around all homes and businesses.

4.42 In this, more than almost any other area of this White Paper, we will only succeed if everyone plays their part:

- local authorities – which provide many of the core environmental services;

- the private sector – which gains significantly from improvements in the quality of the urban environment;

- community and voluntary groups – which can play an active role in management of the urban environment; and

- individuals – whose behaviour can have the biggest impact of all on the quality of the environment.

4.43 In the following sections we set out the action we and others are taking to help improve the management and maintenance of the urban environment including:

- improving the condition of our streets, making them safer and more attractive for pedestrians and cyclists;

- supporting initiatives to improve the quality of our town centres;

- tackling environmental nuisances, like litter, graffiti, fly posting, vandalism, dog fouling, pollution and noise, which can degrade even the most intrinsically attractive places;

- restoring the historic character of our urban environment;

- improving air quality and the global environment; and

- encouraging safe, well designed and managed public open spaces like parks, play areas and recreational areas.

4.44   But these actions will only succeed if they are implemented as part of a broader strategy for maintaining the local environment in each area.

4.45   In its report the Urban Task Force recommended that local authorities should prepare a single strategy for their local environment (or public realm) dealing with provision, design, management, funding and maintenance.

4.46   The Government strongly agrees with the need for a strategic approach to the management and improvement of the local environment. Community Strategies (see Chapter 3, page 33, paragraph 3.15), produced by local authorities and partner organisations, could provide a valuable means to respond to community concerns and priorities on the quality of the local environment.

4.47   The Government also agrees with the House of Commons Environment, Transport and Regional Affairs Select Committee report last year into urban parks which called for action to reverse the decline in our parks and open spaces. As part of our response we are setting in hand a comprehensive programme of work to improve the quality of parks, play-areas and open spaces and to make them cleaner, safer and better maintained. This will be led by a DETR Minister who will oversee the delivery of our proposals (see page 75) and develop a vision for the future of these areas.

4

LOOKING AFTER THE URBAN ENVIRONMENT BETTER
1: Making our streets safer and more attractive

Improving the street environment

1. Streets dominated by traffic not only pose a risk to health and safety but also discourage walking and neighbourliness which can help create a sense of community. The *10 Year Plan for Transport* will contribute to major improvements in the street environment in towns and cities by:

- reducing traffic congestion below current levels by 2010, especially in larger urban areas;

- funding traffic management schemes to reduce noise, nuisance and the severance of communities;

- eliminating the backlog in local road maintenance and street lighting with a £30 billion programme over the next 10 years;

- funding widespread improvements to the provision for cyclists (aimed at trebling cycling by 2010) and schemes to improve the pedestrian environment including safe routes to schools and stations;

- providing cleaner, smarter, high quality public transport facilities like trams and new buses;

- funding Home Zones in residential areas. These seek to make streets places for people, not just traffic. They can provide traffic calming schemes; areas for children to play; or create meeting places for older residents and parents. Nine Home Zones are currently being piloted throughout England and Wales; and

- piloting Clear Zones in town and city centres. They might include car-free or low emission zones; controlled access to town centres; and new services like home delivery. Pilot Clear Zones are due to be selected shortly from the current round of Local Transport Plans. The first should be launched in early 2001.

Dutch Home Zone
(Photograph: Wayne Durden)

2. We will also be taking measures to reduce the disruption caused by street works created by the utilities e.g. water, electricity and telecommunications companies. Initially highway authorities will be able to fine utilities that fail to complete their works by agreed deadlines. If, subsequently, we conclude this has not sufficiently reduced the level of disruption caused we will activate new powers which we are taking in the Transport Bill. These will allow highway authorities to charge utilities from the first day of works (so called "lane rental"). Should we consider it necessary to use these powers, authorities would be able to use proceeds from the scheme to introduce other measures to help reduce the disruption from street works or fund other local transport improvements.

Road safety

3. Since the early 1980s the number of deaths on our roads has fallen by nearly 40% and the number of serious injuries has almost halved. But there are still about 3400 people dying on our roads every year (about one in four of all accidental deaths).

4. In March 2000 we launched a new road safety strategy and set ourselves the challenging target of reducing deaths and serious injuries by 40% by 2010 compared with the 1994-98 average. Within that we want to reduce child deaths and serious injuries by 50%. We also want to see a 10% reduction in the overall rate of slight injuries.

continued

5. With nearly twice as many deaths and serious injuries occurring on roads in built up areas than on the rest of the road network, and over three times the number of slight injuries, we clearly need to see a big improvement in urban areas if we are to meet these targets.

6. Vehicle speed is a factor in many accidents and can make a big difference to the severity of the injuries people suffer. Slowing all traffic is not realistic but we want to see more 20mph zones around schools and in other places where children may be more at risk. In June 1999 we gave local authorities delegated powers to introduce 20mph zones. In addition we are:

- asking local authorities to carry out child road safety audits when reviewing their road safety plans so that they know when, where and why accidents are happening and can develop proposals for future action;

- setting up a pilot project that will help organise a programme of road safety training schemes particularly in deprived areas (responding to research which shows that children from poorer families are five times more likely to be killed in road accidents when out walking than children from other families); and

- investigating why children from minority ethnic groups are also suffering disproportionately from road accident injuries so that we can establish ways of dealing with this directly.

7. More generally we want to see more effective enforcement of existing speed limits on all roads, particularly through the greater use of digital cameras and other new technology including speed-activated warning signs.

LOOKING AFTER THE URBAN ENVIRONMENT BETTER
2: Town centre initiatives

1. The quality of the environment in town and city centres has an important impact on how people see these areas and, in turn, whether they feel comfortable using them. If we are to revitalise town and city centres we need to ensure that they are welcoming, safe and convenient.

2. The Government has already done a great deal to improve the vitality and quality of our town centres in particular through its new Planning Policy Guidance note on town centres and retail developments (see page 45, paragraph 4.25). However it is keen to see the continued development of town centre management more generally and is working with the Association of Town Centre Management (ATCM) to promote good practice.

Town centre management

3. Town centre management aims to bring together property owners, residents, businesses and others with an interest in the future of the town centre to encourage activity and investment. Town centre management partnerships do this by agreeing a shared vision, creating a strategy suited to local needs and implementing an action plan. Many partnerships have employed a town centre manager to co-ordinate their activities.

Town Centre Management Schemes can improve the quality of places by providing a clean and safe environment. (Photograph courtesy of the Association of Town Centre Management)

4. There have already been many successful town centre management schemes in England. 31 local authorities have applied for Beacon status under this year's Town Centre Management theme. But, we believe that more can be done to encourage the private sector to work with the public sector to improve the town centre environment, its security, marketing and promotion.

Town Improvement Schemes (TISs)

5. One way of doing this would be through Town Improvement Schemes (TISs). Drawing on the successful experience of business improvement districts in the United States, these would allow local authorities and local businesses to work together to put in place local projects to improve the area. Projects could cover a wide variety of issues including improvements to the quality of the local environment, the street environment or parks and open spaces.

6. We are currently consulting on proposals for a supplementary business rate in *Modernising Local Government Finance: A Green Paper*. This would provide one mechanism for financing TISs, although views are also sought on alternative funding options.

7. Under the supplementary business rate model, authorities could raise a supplement on the national business rate, where representative partnership arrangements had been agreed with ratepayers. This would be used to pay for local projects chosen in partnership with business ratepayers. There could be a local authority-wide supplement or a locally targeted supplement to support a particular scheme, with the agreement of the affected businesses. The supplementary rate would be limited to 5% of the national rate, phased in at 1% per year. However, high performing authorities may also be able to levy an additional supplementary rate, up to a further 5% in specific targeted areas, subject to the agreement of the ratepayers affected.

LOOKING AFTER THE URBAN ENVIRONMENT BETTER
3: A cleaner local environment

1. A dirty and unpleasant local environment can have a major impact on how an area is viewed and on the quality of life of the people who live in or use it.

2. The Government has already done much to improve the cleanliness and attractiveness of the local environment including:

- published a revised code of practice on litter and refuse which sets out expected standards of cleanliness and response times for when these standards are not met. The code recognises that areas which are used more intensively need more intensive care and requires standards to be maintained in these areas despite their high usage;

- made it a criminal offence to leave or deposit litter, which is subject to a maximum fine of £2,500. In addition, local authorities can appoint litter wardens who can issue £25 Fixed Penalty Notices;

- published a revised Code of Practice to combat fly posting;

- put in place pilot neighbourhood warden and neighbourhood management schemes which, among other issues, will be able to tackle environmental problems such as litter and graffiti;

- introduced Best Value indicators on cleanliness and a "Maintaining a Quality Environment" theme in the Beacon Council Scheme to encourage excellence in areas such as dealing with litter, fly tipping, dog fouling and maintaining high quality street furniture;

- enabled local authorities to make bylaws which require dog owners to keep their dogs on a lead, ban dogs from certain areas in parks, or introduce 'poop scoop' areas where it is an offence not to clear up after your dog; and

- funded Noise Action Day to raise public awareness and understanding of noise and undertaken a review of the Noise Act 1996.

3. There is, however, much that still needs to be done. The Government will:

- work with the Tidy Britain Group, the Local Government Association and others to introduce a more targeted and comprehensive approach to the problem of littering. This will be designed to:

  – improve the education of young people to reduce the amount of litter dropped;

  – take a more rigourous approach to dealing with littering offences, and

  – set a good example by keeping streets clean and free from litter.

  We will also be working with the Tidy Britain Group to develop a better system for measuring cleanliness standards and using the Best Value regime and Beacon Council Scheme to share best practice and deal with councils that are performing poorly.

- review existing guidance on designing out crime and issue new guidance (see Chapter 6, page 120); and

- issue good practice guidance to local authorities on the use of powers to clean up land adversely affecting the amenity of a neighbourhood with the aim of reducing the number of eyesores.

4. An additional source of funds which may shortly be made available to local communities throughout the UK to help improve this and other aspects of their local environment is the New Opportunities Fund's proposed Transforming Communities programme. Part of this programme, which, subject to consultation, would be worth over £150m over three years, could help communities undertake improvements to the appearance of their local environment. Projects might include improvements to specific physical features such as public open spaces, the quality and design of the street environment, local heritage features, or the removal of eyesores. The programme could help repair the minor tears in the urban fabric as envisaged by Lord Rogers when he proposed the Renaissance Fund.

Litter can often seriously detract from the urban environment.
(Photograph: Ken Kay, courtesy of Tidy Britain Group)

4

LOOKING AFTER THE URBAN ENVIRONMENT BETTER
4: The historic environment

1. Historic buildings, parks and open spaces make a great contribution to the character, diversity and sense of identity of urban areas. Small-scale improvements to the historic fabric of an area can generate a market-led return to urban living, supporting existing communities and adding to the economic base.

2. English Heritage is the Government's adviser on all matters concerning the conservation of England's historic environment. Its nine regional offices advise owners, developers and government on managing changes to improve the historic environment. 60% of the £35m they offer each year in grants for conservation work is aimed at regeneration schemes, targeted on urgent repairs to the fabric of historic areas, buildings, parks and gardens. English Heritage's new Heritage Economic Regeneration Schemes invest £18m in under-used retail premises and run-down public areas. By funding repairs and environmental improvements and the reuse of empty upper floors for new homes, these schemes are attracting back key workers and others to live near their work in urban centres.

3. Urban renewal is also a key objective of the Heritage Lottery Fund, particularly in its Urban Parks and Townscape Heritage Initiatives. By the end of 2002 the Urban Parks Initiative will have provided £255m to restore and improve parks and gardens in the UK. The Townscape Heritage Initiative has already allocated £62m for the regeneration of historic towns and cities across the UK including many in deprived areas.

4. At the Government's request English Heritage is currently carrying out a wide-ranging consultation on the existing policies and systems for managing and protecting our historic buildings and other parts of the built heritage. They will report on the first stage of this Historic Environment Policy Review later this year and there will be a major policy statement from the Government on the Historic Environment in 2001.

5. As announced in the November 2000 Pre-Budget Report, the Government is also intending to explore with the European Commission the scope for reducing VAT for listed buildings that are places of worship as another step in helping to restore our national heritage. The Government has already written to the Commission to make its position clear.

6. English Heritage's publication *The Heritage Dividend* demonstrates clearly the way that refurbishment of the historic fabric can act as a catalyst for wider regeneration, tackling social exclusion and building communities. It estimates that for every £10,000 spent, £48,000 of match funding is levered in from other private and public sources, generating and safeguarding jobs, creating new homes and improving other facilities.

English Heritage's investment of £550,000 in repair, restoration and environmental improvements was a major catalyst for the transformation of Brixton town centre into a thriving 24 hour economy, drawing in almost £2m of additional public and private investment and safeguarding 120 local jobs.
(Photograph: Boris Baggs, courtesy of English Heritage)

LOOKING AFTER THE URBAN ENVIRONMENT BETTER
5: Air quality and climate change

Air quality

1. The quality of our air is a particularly important measure of local environmental quality. Air pollution has a direct effect on people's health and hits hardest the most vulnerable in our society – the old, the very young and the deprived, and in particular those suffering from asthma or heart and lung diseases.

2. Much has already been done to reduce the impacts of industry and road transport on air quality. Improved pollution control regulations have significantly reduced permitted emissions from many sectors of industry. And improvements in vehicle technology and fuel quality have substantially reduced vehicle emissions. By 2010 emissions of pollutants from road traffic should be less than half their 1997 levels.

3. But while air quality in towns and cities has improved considerably in the last decade it is still a serious problem. On current projections, the improvements in vehicle emissions will begin to reverse beyond 2010 unless traffic growth reduces. There are many urban areas where more needs to be done before air quality objectives are met.

4. We have put in place a system of local air quality management giving all local authorities a duty to assess and review local conditions. Measures to tackle air quality which falls below certain standards might include the use of traffic regulation orders to restrict traffic in certain areas or at certain times. The substantial increase in transport investment in the *10 Year Plan for Transport*, for both public transport schemes and local traffic management schemes, will help deliver further improvements in air quality. And we are encouraging organisations, in both the public and private sectors, to put together travel plans to promote walking, cycling, the use of public transport and car sharing. We expect local authorities to set a good example by adopting travel plans and using cleaner fuelled vehicles.

Climate change

5. Climate change is one of the greatest envrionmental threats facing the world today. Left unchecked, it could have far-reaching effects on all aspects of our society.

6. Because of their concentration of people, industry, houses and activity, urban areas are main contributors to the greenhouse gases that cause climate change. The way in which our urban areas develop in the future will greatly affect emission levels. The UK's climate change programme, which will be published shortly, will set out how businesses, local authorities and people can all help to reduce emissions by, for example, using more fuel efficient cars, travelling by car a little less, making their businesses and their homes more energy efficient, and investing in new forms of electricity generation.

7. The Government-sponsored UK Climate Impacts Programme is helping regions, local authorities and business assess their vulnerability to the impacts of climate change and prepare plans for adapting to it. We are also now strengthening Planning Policy Guidance to take more account of environmental hazards such as flooding, and we shall issue a good practice guide on the implications of climate change for the planning process.

4

LOOKING AFTER THE URBAN ENVIRONMENT BETTER
6: Parks, play areas and public spaces

1. Well-managed public open spaces such as greens, squares, parks, children's play areas, allotments, woodlands and recreational and sporting areas improve the attractiveness of urban areas and help promote a healthier lifestyle. They, and other spaces such as agricultural and horticultural businesses, bring benefits for wildlife and the environment, act as an important educational tool and can relieve pressure on the countryside. They are therefore vital to enhancing the quality of urban environments and the quality of our lives.

2. We want everyone to have access to well-maintained and safe parks, play areas and other open spaces close to where they live and work. For many people, such spaces will be provided within the town or city, but for some, these spaces may be more accessible on the urban fringe and in the countryside. We continue to value green belts around towns and cities as the current Government's record demonstrates: since 1997 an additional 30,000 hectares of green belt has been designated or proposed. The Rural White Paper considers in more detail the role of the countryside around towns and the challenges faced by agricultural businesses in these areas.

3. Over the last few decades a lot of public open space within urban areas has been lost to encroaching development and too much of what is left has been neglected and poorly maintained. Last year's report on public parks by the House of Commons Environment, Transport and Regional Affairs Select Committee raised concerns over the future of our parks and called for action to reverse the decline. We share the Committee's concerns about the state of parks and open spaces, and agree that some aspects of the way in which they are managed and maintained need to be improved.

4. Action already being taken to help includes:

- **new sources of funding** – by the end of 2002, £96m from the New Opportunities Fund Green

Spaces and Sustainable Communities Programme will have been made available to create and improve green spaces which are of importance to local communities in England. £255m will also have been made available from the Heritage Lottery Fund Urban Parks Programme (see page 72, paragraph 3);

- **preventing the loss of school playing fields** – by making it necessary for all state schools to get the approval of the Secretary of State for Education to change the use of any field which has been used for sports in the last five years. DETR has a new power to call in for Ministerial decision planning applications for development of such playing fields where it would result in a shortage of playing fields for the wider community and where Sport England have objected to the application. Since adopting these measures, the number of disposals has dropped from 40 to only three a month;

- **raising standards of local services** – encouraging improvements in the quality of service standards in the provision and management of parks and open spaces by local authorities through the Best Value regime; and

- **taking environmental action** – by enabling and funding environmental and voluntary groups such as the Groundwork Federation, the British Trust for Conservation Volunteers (BTCV), and Wildlife Trusts to take action to improve the quality of local environments. We will continue to support such groups through a number of initiatives including the Environmental Action Fund, the Special Grants Programme, and the Environment Task Force option of the New Deal.

continued

Alexandra Park in Stockport – a *Green Flag Park Awards* winner in 1999/2000 – is a formal Edwardian park, extended in 1990, close to popular local shopping and other local facilities. It includes woodland, garden and recreation areas including tennis courts, a basket ball court, bowling greens and a crazy golf area. The park also has a pavillion for community activities and is used as a base by the Community Involvement Rangers.

(Photograph courtesy of Stockport Metropolitan Borough Council/Green Flag Park Steering Group/The Civic Trust)

5. But we must do more than simply halt the decline. The challenge for us all is to find ways of improving the quality of parks, play areas and open spaces and make them cleaner, safer and better-maintained places. We need to think more imaginatively about the kind of open spaces that can make a difference to the quality of people's lives in urban settings. We will take action in three key areas.

We must lead and develop a shared vision for the future of our parks, play areas and open spaces.

- A DETR Minister will be directly responsible for overseeing the development of a vision and proposals for the sorts of parks, play areas and open spaces we want to see created in the future and how they should be managed. The Minister will also oversee the delivery of our proposals below, and the development of a number of demonstation projects that show how our vision for parks, play areas and open spaces can be achieved.

- We will appoint an 'Advisory Committee', which will be chaired by the Minister, to advise and assist the conduct of this work. The Committee will:

  – review evidence of the current state of parks, play areas and open spaces and the ways in which they are managed and maintained;

  – consider how different types of open spaces can best meet the needs of people in urban areas;

  – examine innovation in the design, creation and maintenance of open spaces in different areas of this country and in other countries.

- We will identify opportunities for building and supporting partnerships for managing public open spaces and the countryside in and around towns and cities, in particular, those involving local business, including agricultural businesses, and resident communities.

We must improve information on the quality and quantity of parks and open spaces, and the way in which they are used and maintained. We will:

- improve the comprehensiveness of the database of local authority parks being developed jointly by Heritage Lottery Fund, English Heritage and DETR;

- commission a programme of research to:

  – examine ways in which parks and open spaces are used and by whom, what users want from them, what they currently provide, and their wider benefits to the quality of urban environments;

4

– examine roles and responsibilities in relation to managing and improving the public realm; and

- assess alternative approaches to managing and maintaining the public realm, in particular, public open spaces and approaches involving the local community and business groups.

We must also improve the way we plan and design new parks, play areas and public spaces, and the way we manage and maintain existing ones. We will:

- in partnership with the Urban Parks Forum, develop a programme for identifying and spreading good practice on the management and care of parks, play areas and open spaces to parks staff, professionals and user groups;

- develop the Green Flags Awards scheme as a national award for excellence in the provision, management and care of parks, children's play areas and open spaces (along the lines of the European Blue Flag awards for beaches). The scheme will also help to define and promote quality service standards;

- revise *Planning Policy Guidance Note 17: Sports and Recreation* to give local planning authorities a clearer framework for assessing their needs for open spaces, making good deficiencies and protecting what is valued, and ensuring that everyone has adequate access to open space. It will also aim to ensure that existing spaces are protected from development where appropriate and that new open spaces are well designed; and

- work with a range of partners including the Countryside Agency, LGA, Civic Trust and Groundwork UK to develop proposals for raising awareness of the importance of caring for parks, play areas and public spaces and places (including town and local centres), encouraging 'local champions' and identifying opportunities for involving local people in looking after local places and spaces better.

Creating and sharing prosperity

The Government's aim is for all towns and cities to be economically successful: identifying and building on their economic strengths; encouraging enterprise and innovation across society; providing employment opportunities for all; and promoting lifelong learning so they have a flexible and adaptable workforce.

Contents

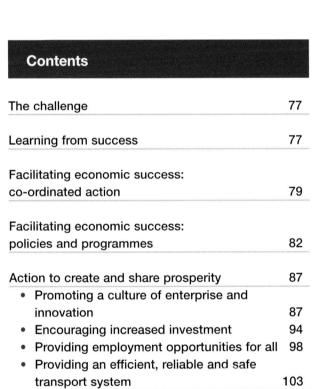

The challenge

5.1 Successful towns and cities have always been at the heart of economic development and the creation of prosperity whether as market places or as centres of enterprise, knowledge, culture, learning and innovation. Our economy depends on their success.

5.2 We want all urban areas to achieve their economic potential and enjoy sustainable growth and rising prosperity.

5.3 We also want to ensure a fairer sharing of prosperity. Wealth and opportunity often exist side by side with poverty and isolation. We must make good use of the diverse skills and backgrounds of all people, enabling everyone to fulfil their potential and excluding no one. This is important if we are to create a caring and inclusive society and, in particular, to achieve the Government's key commitment to abolish child poverty in 20 years and halve it in 10 years. It also makes sound economic sense as it will help to increase the long term growth potential of the economy.

Learning from success

5.4 Chapters 1 and 2 outlined the massive changes – economic, technological, environmental and social – to which our towns and cities have had to respond in recent decades. Some places have been more successful than others in adapting to these changes. We need to learn from them so we can create the conditions in which all areas can be successful and can continue to adapt to change.

5

Leeds

Leeds is a prosperous city and one of the fastest growing centres in Europe for job creation. Over 40,000 jobs were created between 1991 and 1998 with forecasts suggesting that a further 48,000 jobs will be created in the next decade. Finance and business services are expected to account for 85% of net employment growth.

Although the numbers employed in manufacturing have declined, Leeds is still the third largest manufacturing centre outside London. There are 56,400 employed in manufacturing which represents 16% of total employment in Leeds.

As well as being one of Yorkshire's important commercial centres, Leeds is also one of the region's cultural centres. The city has a lively arts, sporting and entertainment scene and boasts both new and refurbished theatres – Opera North and the West Yorkshire Playhouse are based in the city.

Recent regeneration programmes and lottery grants, including an award of over £5m from the Millennium Commission have focused on the restoration of the city centre. Hotels, galleries and cafe bars can now be found together with award-winning architecture. The city attracts over 20 million visitors a year spending £587m in 1998. Between 1994 and 1998 overseas visitor volume and spending increased by 75%.

Leeds is a good example of a city moving forward. There are still considerable problems in areas like education and income levels with examples of prosperity and poverty in close proximity. These must be tackled if Leeds is to continue its success in the future. Regeneration partners in Leeds recognise the need to generate growth and tackle social exclusion together. Leeds is a positive example other cities could learn from.

5.5   Successful places need to be able to attract and retain businesses, based on understanding their requirements. The following table sets out the results of a survey which asked EU companies about the key factors which influence their location decisions.

Essential factors for locating business (EU companies)

Factor	% companies
Easy access to markets, customer or clients	66
Transport links with other cities and internationally	62
The quality of telecommunications	54
Cost and availability of staff	50
The climate governments create for business	36
Value for money of office space	26
Availability of office space	25
Languages spoken	22
Ease of travelling within the city	21
The quality of life for employees	13
Freedom from pollution	12

Source: Healey and Baker (1998) *European Cities Monitor*

5.6   An analysis of successful and less successful places suggests several factors which are crucial to the economic prosperity of towns and cities. There is a strong overlap between these factors and those listed in the above table as influencing business location decisions.

5.7   This chapter discusses the following four factors that are key to economic success:

- **A culture of enterprise and innovation** – where places adapt quickly to new opportunities and everyone can share in the possibilities and rewards of business success. This includes embracing the opportunities presented by the revolution in information and communications technology.

- **Private investment, including access to venture capital** – essential for businesses to start up and grow, and to deliver jobs and opportunity for all.

- **People equipped with the skills employers need, and with motivation and opportunity to work** – a culture of life-long learning enabling people to fulfil their potential and maximising employment opportunities; enabling a flexible response to changing opportunities; and encouraging companies to come to, and remain in, towns and cities.

- **An efficient and reliable transport system** – enabling efficient delivery of raw materials to industry and of goods to market; providing access to jobs; making towns and cities better places to live in; and helping tackle social exclusion.

Stratford station on the extended Jubilee Line.
The extended Jubilee Line is helping to provide access to jobs and regenerate a large area of south and east London.

5.8 Economic success is also underpinned by a range of other factors discussed elsewhere in this White Paper.

- **Alert and pro-active local authorities and Regional Development Agencies** ready and willing to respond to the needs of business. (Chapter 3)

- **A well designed and managed physical environment**, including housing and local amenities – providing an efficient, attractive and safe environment within which to live and work. (Chapter 4)

- **Good quality services and cultural and leisure opportunities** – attracting businesses and people, and making them want to stay. (Chapter 6)

5.9 We want to encourage business-led growth and opportunity for all by working in partnership with business and regional and local bodies to create these conditions for success in all urban areas.

Facilitating economic success: co-ordinated action

5.10 The economic success or failure of a town or city has an impact well beyond its administrative boundaries. It influences the prosperity of the surrounding area. The major conurbations influence the entire region and make a key contribution to the national economy. Conversely the surrounding areas have a significant impact on the quality of life of towns and cities.

Brixton, London
Thriving towns and cities make a key contribution to the national economy.
(Photograph: Richard Townshend)

5.11 The performance of towns and cities is a major component of the success of the national economy as a whole. They in turn are influenced by the performance of the rest of the economy and the fiscal and other measures taken by Government to manage the national economy.

5.12 At the regional and local level, market towns across the country also perform a vital role for their surrounding rural areas. The Rural White Paper addresses how we can boost this aspect of a town's function.

5.13 Given these inter-relationships it is essential that action at the national, regional, local and neighbourhood level is closely co-ordinated and mutually reinforcing. This section looks at the roles and responsibilities of bodies at each level and how they need to fit together.

National action

5.14 National Government has the responsibility for establishing a macro-economic framework that supports a strong and stable economy.

The macro-economic framework

5.15 The UK has a history of poor economic performance in comparison with other G7 economies. Much of this can be attributed to macro-economic policy errors in the past. The Government has introduced new frameworks for both monetary and fiscal policy, designed to avoid a repeat of the mistakes which led to boom and bust cycles. In the past these cycles have been enormously damaging to the UK economy. For example, each downturn has led to more people becoming detached from the labour market.

5.16 The new frameworks are delivering significant benefits. The UK economy has enjoyed a period of stability and steady growth; inflation has remained close to target; and employment has risen to record levels. The latest available data show a UK employment rate of 74.7% (June to August 2000). This is the the highest since Spring 1990 and the second highest in the EU.

5.17 The chart below shows a stabilisation of the business cycle. It plots the output gap – the difference between the long-term capacity of the economy and the actual level of output. A negative output gap represents output above the trend level – the recession of the late 1980s is represented by a high positive output gap. The chart demonstrates reduced fluctuations from the trend level in recent years.

The Output Gap

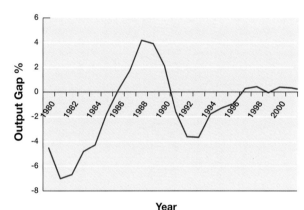

Year

Source: HM Treasury estimates: Pre-Budget Report 8 November 2000.

5.18 A stable economy with low inflation helps businesses and individuals plan for the longer term. This in turn encourages investment, both in physical assets and in the skills and development of the workforce. Both of these help raise productivity.

Policies and programmes to support growth

5.19 The Government also needs to establish policies and programmes to help create the conditions for business-led growth.

5.20 The important role of Government, and DETR and DTI in particular, is reflected in the joint DETR/DTI Public Service Agreement (PSA) target "to raise the economic performance of all regions as measured by the rate of growth in the regions' GDP per head."

5.21 Pages 87 to 104 below summarise the action we have already taken and the new measures we are now proposing.

Regional Strategies

5.22 At the regional level the responsibility for producing a Regional Strategy rests with the Regional Development Agencies (RDAs) outside London and with the London Development Agency. They are at the heart of the Government's agenda for promoting sustainable regional economic growth, enterprise and regeneration, working in partnership with the Regional Chambers, Regional Planning Bodies and others.

5.23 The RDAs have five statutory purposes, to:

- further the economic development and the regeneration of their area;

- promote business efficiency, investment and competitiveness in their area;

- promote employment in their area;

- enhance the development and application of skills relevant to employment in their area; and

- contribute to the achievement of sustainable development in the UK.

5.24 The RDAs:

- influence the way in which central government polices and programmes are developed and implemented to maximise their contribution to the region's economic objectives;

- undertake major regeneration projects, improve physical infrastructure and help others to regenerate their local areas;

- promote their region abroad to attract inward investment (including EC funding), international networks and trade;

- support businesses and promote innovation and cluster development;

- work with the new local Learning and Skills Council, business sector groups and national training organisations to ensure that skills training matches the needs of the labour market; and

- work with higher education regional associations and individual higher education institutions to optimise higher education's contribution to urban regeneration.

5.25 In the Spending Review 2000 the Government announced that the RDAs would have a strengthened role as strategic leaders of economic development, promoting innovation and enterprise in the regions. Their combined budget will rise from £1.2 billion this year to £1.7 billion in 2003/04. From April 2002 the separate budgets from DETR, DfEE and DTI will be brought together in a Single Budget, giving the RDAs much greater flexibility to use the money they are allocated where it can have the greatest impact.

5.26 The Government welcomes the RDAs' enthusiasm in developing the Single Budget and has decided to take a major step towards this from April 2001 through introducing:

- **more budgetary flexibility.** RDAs will be allowed to transfer up to 20% of any programme into any other programme, so long as it is consistent with their delivery objectives; and

- **a new Strategic Programme.** RDAs will be able to switch resources into a new Strategic Programme for innovative schemes that meet their economic and other strategic aims. This Strategic Programme will be a test-bed for the Single Budget, with new project and appraisal processes.

5.27 RDAs will also be asked to develop stretching outcome and output targets to demonstrate that they are achieving their strategic goals.

Local action

5.28 As explained in Chapter 3, the key to delivering effective action at the local level is the development of a tailor-made Community Strategy by a Local Strategic Partnership, involving local businesses, local authorities, community groups and other key stakeholders. The new duty to promote race equality will give added impetus to the need to ensure that ethnic minority communities are fully engaged in this.

5.29 Sustainable economic development should be a central element of every Community Strategy, building as appropriate on the existing business base. The Local Strategic Partnership should carefully assess the economic situation of their area to build up a better understanding of the economic portfolio they offer businesses.

5.30 They then need to formulate a strategy which capitalises on their assets and opportunities and addresses any weaknesses or threats. In doing this they should regard the Government's policies and programmes as building blocks, and agree with key service providers how they should be used to produce the best overall result for the local area.

5.31 Sustainable economic development is a key local driver for tackling deprivation and securing urban renaissance. Alongside local authorities, RDAs will therefore be key members of Local Strategic Partnerships (LSPs) in areas where they are seeking to deliver economic regeneration. Of course economic and social regeneration go hand in hand, and that is why both the private sector and communities will have a strong voice on LSPs.

Local economic development

Plymouth has had an overarching multi-sector partnership since 1993. Gaining *New Commitment to Regeneration* pathfinder status, the partnership re-launched itself as *Plymouth 2020*. The partnership oversees the city's area based initiatives which include: a health action zone, education action zone, employment zone and community legal service partnership. The New Commitment partnership is a catalyst to harmonise planning and time-tabling of all area-based initiatives in the city.

(Photograph: Richard Townshend)

5

Facilitating economic success: policies and programmes

5.32   The rest of this chapter explains the policies and programmes we have put or are putting in place in four key areas:

- Promoting a culture of enterprise and innovation.

- Encouraging increased investment.

- Providing employment opportunities for all.

- Providing an efficient, reliable and safe transport system.

5.33   Paragraphs 5.34–5.54 set out the issues and the Government's approach. The shaded pages at the end of the chapter (pages 87-104) provide more detail on the policies and programmes. The relevant Public Serice Agreements are on page 86.

Promoting a culture of enterprise and innovation

5.34   Within the context of a stable economy, our approach is based on business-led growth. This is supported at the national level by policies and programmes aimed at removing barriers which hinder investment and prevent an enterprise and innovation culture for all.

5.35   Recent evidence from the *Global Entrepreneurship Monitor* (1999) suggests that UK enterprise compares well with much of Europe, but lags behind some of its other leading competitors in providing the right environment and culture to support entrepreneurial activity.

- Entrepreneurial activity in the UK (planning to start a business and investing directly in such enterprises) is around half that of the most entrepreneurial country, the US.

- The UK is more risk averse in relation to entrepreneurship than any other G7 country except Japan.

- Only 16% of people in the UK think that good entrepreneurial opportunities exist compared to 57% in the US.

- The UK has lower levels of entrepreneurial activity among women – 2% of women are trying to start a business compared to 5% of men. By comparison, the figures in the US are 7% and 10% respectively.

5.36   In addition, there are significant differences in business start-up rates across the regions of the UK and within the regions. One of the best measures available for business start-ups is the number of VAT registrations per 10,000 resident population. This varies widely across local authority districts: small businesses' VAT registrations were six times higher in high employment areas than in those with high unemployment.

5.37   We want to promote a culture of enterprise and innovation across society by:

- creating the conditions in which new and existing businesses can thrive;

- encouraging enterprise across society;

- stimulating innovation through capitalising on the knowledge base of research institutions;

- encouraging support for cluster development; and

- creating the right environment for e-business to prosper.

Encouraging increased investment

5.38   As mentioned in the *Global Entrepreneurship Monitor* evidence above, the UK has low levels of investment in new enterprises. The Government is now reversing the UK's record of under-investment. Greater macroeconomic stability, lower long-term interest rates and structural reforms designed to raise productivity have together helped to create a much-improved environment for investment. As a result, business investment as a share of GDP reached record levels in 1999, with continued strong investment this year.

5.39   The Government is taking additional steps to build on this success. We will further increase flows of private investment, helping enterprises across all sectors develop their potential, by:

- encouraging the availability of risk finance; and

- providing a range of measures to stimulate enterprise and wealth creation in under-invested communities including new commitments announced in the Pre-Budget Report in response to the recommendations of the Social Investment Task Force.

Providing employment opportunities for all

5.40 Focus on the labour market has in the past tended to be on unemployment, particularly claimant unemployment. Historically there have been long-standing differences in the unemployment rates of different regions. For example, the North was particularly badly hit in the recession of the early 1980s, while the recovery in the late 1980s was largely concentrated in the South of England. But in the last few years, the differences between the regions that opened up during the 1980s have narrowed. This is shown in the table below.

Largest difference in claimant count rates between regions*

	(percentage points)
National peak in unemployment (July 1986)	9.5
Last trough in unemployment (May 1990)	10.1
Last peak in unemployment (December 1992)	5.6
Latest figures (September 2000)	3.9

* Standard Statistical Regions
Source: Benefits Agency administrative system

5.41 The table shows the difference between the highest and lowest claimant count rates across regions. The figures illustrate that there was a large divergence – 10.1 percentage points – between regions following the recovery in the late 1980s. This gap has now narrowed considerably to 3.9 percentage points.

5.42 However such a narrow focus does not adequately capture complexities of the labour market. The Government has therefore changed the emphasis towards employment as the key labour market indicator – this enables us to take into account people who are inactive, i.e. those not on benefits or seeking work.

5.43 The table below shows that all regions have areas of high and low employment rates. Employment variations are greater within regions than between regions.

Employment rate variations within regions

Region	Average Employment rate	Range of employment rates in Region	Range within Region (% points)
EU15 (1999)	64.2		
UK (Apr-June 2000)	74.6		
South East	80.9	67.3 – 89.3	21.9
South West	78.7	61.7 – 89.7	27.9
Eastern	78.5	67.5 – 85.9	18.4
East Midlands	77.0	63.1 – 87.1	24.0
Yorks & Humber	74.1	63.2 – 86.9	23.7
West Midlands	73.8	64.6 – 86.5	21.9
North West	73.2	57.7 – 86.5	28.8
London	70.8	58.0 – 84.1	26.1
North East	68.7	56.3 – 83.9	27.7
Range (% points)	12.2		

Source: *Labour Force Survey*. Unitary/local authority district data are 1999 DfEE estimates

5.44 Job vacancies arise across the country all the time. Employers notify around 2.75 million vacancies to Government Jobcentres in the UK each year; and we estimate that Jobcentre vacancies represent around a third of total vacancies. The range of types of jobs available in the UK is much wider than elsewhere in the EU. This tends to enable a wider range of people find a pattern of work which suits their circumstances.

5.45 Although a range of employment opportunities arise all the time, joblessness is concentrated among certain groups and in certain localities in both urban and rural areas. The areas of low employment rates tend to be where the numbers on welfare – both unemployment related and other benefits – are highest. Often these areas face multiple disadvantages.

5.46 A key aim of Government policy is to tackle this inequality in employment opportunities. Providing employment opportunities for all is the single most effective means of tackling poverty and social exclusion. Employment enables individuals to improve their living standards; it also makes constructive use of human resources. In a modern economy, countries that succeed will be those that get the best out of all their people.

5

5.47 We want towns and cities where residents can share in higher living standards through employment. Individuals not in employment must be willing to take advantage of employment opportunities; and employers must be willing to consider the widest range of people for the jobs on offer. We want to deliver a better quality of life for all by changing the welfare culture to one built on work and security – work for those who can; and security for those who cannot.

5.48 The Government vision is for people to have the skills, motivation and opportunity to make the most of their employment potential. We are:

- raising education standards to equip young people to be able to take up jobs;

- assisting unemployed people to acquire employability skills and find work largely through the New Deals for unemployed claimants;

- developing a culture of lifelong learning which makes for a flexible and adaptable workforce;

- making work pay and easing the transition into work, through tax and benefit reforms;

- helping parents balance work with their family lives, further education and training more effectively and with greater confidence;

- providing high quality, affordable and accessible childcare and early education; and

- helping people on inactive benefits back into the labour market and into employment through various welfare to work initiatives.

5.49 At regional and local level, national policies are supplemented by geographically specific policies. The Government has developed a wide range of local initiatives designed to improve the functioning of regional and local product and labour markets. Examples include Employment Zones, New Deal for Communities and the suite of regional policies which include Regional Selective Assistance.

Providing an efficient, reliable and safe transport system

5.50 At the national level the Government has embarked on a major new long-term programme of investment to modernise and upgrade this country's transport networks.

5.51 Over the last twenty years road traffic in Great Britain has grown by over 70%. This growth in traffic has led to increasing congestion on the road network. The table below shows that congestion is a problem faced particularly in urban areas.

Road Congestion

	All Areas	London	Conurbations and Large Urban	Other urban	Other
Index of time lost per km	100	367	212	98	35

Source: Transport 2010 The Background Analysis, July 2000, DETR

5.52 In many towns and cities public transport does not provide an attractive option:

- Outside London, only 15% of those working in metropolitan areas, and 7% in other towns, commute by public transport.

- In London, where around 75% of those working in the central area travel to work by public transport, there are problems of overcrowding in peak times on the Underground, and four out of ten London commuter rail services exceed overcrowding standards.

- Inadequate public transport also contributes to problems of social exclusion, since people in the poorest households, the elderly, and young people are more reliant on public transport.

5.53 In response to these challenges, the *10 Year Transport Plan* announced our commitment to a £180 billion programme of public and private investment by 2010. This will ensure:

- a reduction in congestion and better maintained roads;

- a step change in quality of public transport;

- improved access to groups who are heavily reliant on public transport, such as children, older people and those with disabilities; and

- better access to jobs and services, including from deprived areas.

The Midland Metro
The *10 Year Transport Plan* includes provision for up to 25 new light rail lines in major cities and conurbations, to more than double light rail use by 2010.
(Photograph: Richard Townshend)

5.54 At the regional level major transport investment is being co-ordinated through the new Regional Transport Strategies (RTSs) as an integral part of Regional Planning Guidance. These strategies should, amongst other things, contribute to regional prosperity and help facilitate the delivery of the RDA regional strategies which have such a key role in this.

5.55 The following box sets out the key Public Service Agreements which are relevant to creating and sharing prosperity in towns and cities. These challenging targets will ensure public resources are used in the most effective way to maximise the economic potential of towns and cities. Pages 87-104 set out the policies and programmes we have put and are putting in place to provide the building blocks for economic success.

Key Public Service Agreements relevant to creating and sharing prosperity

Enterprise and innovation

- Improve UK competitiveness by narrowing the productivity gap with US, France, Germany and Japan over the economic cycle. (HMT/DTI)

- Help build an enterprise society in which small firms of all kinds thrive and achieve their potential, with an increase in the number of people considering going into business, an improvement in the overall productivity of small firms, and more enterprise in disadvantaged communities. (DTI)

- Make and keep the UK the best place in the world to trade electronically, as measured by the cost of Internet access and the extent of business to business and business to consumer transactions carried out over e-commerce networks. (DTI)

- Improve the economic performance of all regions measured by trend in growth of each region's GDP per capita. (DTI/DETR)

- Increase the level of exploitation of technological knowledge derived from the science and engineering base, as demonstrated by a significant rise in the proportion of innovating businesses citing such sources. (DTI)

Investment

- Maintain the UK as the prime location in the EU for foreign direct investment. (DTI/FCO)

- Improve the economic performance of all regions measured by trend in growth of each region's GDP per capita. (DTI/DETR)

continued

5

Key Public Service Agreements relevant to creating and sharing prosperity *continued*

Employment opportunities

- By 2004, increase by 3% the numbers of 19 year olds achieving a qualification equivalent to National Vocational Qualification level 2 compared to 2002. (DfEE)

- In Higher Education, while maintaining standards:

  - Increase participation towards 50% of those aged 18 – 30 by the end of the decade;

  - Make significant year on year progress towards fair access, as measured by the Funding Council benchmarks; and

  - Bear down on rates of non-completion. (DfEE)

- Reduce the number of adults who have literacy or numeracy problems by 750,000 by 2004. (DfEE)

- Over the 3 years to 2004, increase the employment rates of disadvantaged areas and groups, taking account of the economic cycle – people with disabilities, lone parents, ethnic minorities and the over 50s, the 30 local authority districts with the poorest initial labour market position – and reduce the difference between their employment rates and the overall rate. (DfEE)

- Make substantial progress towards eradicating child poverty by reducing the number of children in poverty by at least a quarter by 2004. (HMT/DSS)

- Reduce the number of children in households with no-one in work over the 3 years to 2004. (DfEE)

Transport

- Reduce road congestion in large urban areas below current levels by 2010 by promoting integrated transport solutions and investing in public transport and the road network. (DETR)

- Increase bus use from 2000 levels by 10% by 2010, while improving punctuality and reliability. (DETR)

- Double light rail use from 2000 levels by 2010. (DETR)

- Reduce the number of people killed or seriously injured in GB in road accidents by 40% by 2010 and the number of children killed or seriously injured by 50% compared with the average for 1994-98. (DETR)

- Increase rail use in Great Britain by 50% between 2000 and 2010, while improving punctuality and reliability. (DETR)

- Cut journey times on London Underground by increasing capacity and reducing delays. (DETR)

[1] Extracted from Objectives and Performance targets published following Spending Review 2000

ACTION TO CREATE AND SHARE PROSPERITY
1. Promoting a culture of enterprise and innovation

1. We want to promote a culture of enterprise and innovation in order to:

- widen prosperity, promoting and sustaining people's interest in the possibilities and rewards of enterprise, and encouraging more people to go into business – including people who might not immediately think that enterprise is for them;

- help towns and cities adapt creatively to change, embracing new business opportunities including those presented by the revolution in information and communications technology.

Adapting to change: Huddersfield, the creative town

More and more towns and cities are discovering the value of creative and sporting industries to economic success. Huddersfield is just one example of a place which is adapting to changes in its economic base by developing a new focus on creative industries.

The Huddersfield Creative Town Initiative is a four year EU pilot project which will show how creativity can be nurtured in individuals and in a whole town. Its main focus is on new media, but it embraces all arts activity. It works by tapping into and developing people's creativity to tackle issues such as training, business development and enterprise. It produces hard, practical ideas which are networked, circulated and transformed into products and services which are marketable.

Already the initiative has created and safeguarded more than 300 jobs, trained more than 6500 people, created almost 50 new work-spaces, helped develop more than 20 new products and assisted almost 400 businesses.

Encouraging enterprise across society

2. We want all members of society to have the opportunity to make full use of their talents. In order to encourage enterprise across society, in April 2000 we set up the **Small Business Service** (SBS). Its agenda includes:

- working with new and existing small and medium-sized businesses to ensure their varied and diverse needs can be met and their potential realised;

- improving the quality and coherence of support to such businesses, through a new network of 45 Business Links and a new national information and advice service including on-line access;

- acting as a strong voice for small businesses at the heart of Government ensuring that barriers to enterprise are identified and overcome.

3. Business growth and start-ups can provide a means to sustained economic development and improved prosperity in all areas, including our poorest urban areas. In response to work on developing the National Strategy for Neighbourhood Renewal we have already:

- given the **SBS** a clear remit to promote enterprise in deprived areas and among groups that are under-represented in business, including women and some ethnic minorities. This remit is being built into the delivery plans of the new Business Links;

- created a new **£30m Phoenix Fund**, managed by the Small Business Service, to invest over three years in promoting better access to business support and finance. The fund was more than trebled through Spending Review 2000;

continued

- appointed DTI Minister Kim Howells MP as the **Minister for Corporate Social Responsibility** (CSR) to help make the business case for business engagement in corporate social responsibility, and to improve the co-ordination of activity across Whitehall to promote CSR;

- announced that we will fund the SBS to work with the RDAs, Local Strategic Partnerships and others on developing **City Growth Strategies** which will map the economic asset base and develop detailed action plans for business growth in a number of core cities over three years. These will help cities build on their often-overlooked competitive advantages and expand their existing business base.

Connecticut Inner City Business Strategy Initiative – a local partnership approach

In Connecticut US state leaders mobilised teams of over 200 business, civic and community leaders to create growth strategies in five inner-city areas. Together, they have identified the economic competitive advantages inherent in each inner-city area and the business clusters that make up their economy; and built city-specific, fact-based action plans for business growth that can create jobs, income and wealth for local residents.

Many of the resulting initiatives are well on their way to producing visible results. For example:

- the proposed Hartford Enterprise Partnership will provide a range of business advice services to inner-city companies;

- in Bridgeport, the Metal Manufacturers' Education and Training Alliance, a private sector-led cluster work group, will help to boost the competitiveness of the metal manufacturing industry; and

- New Haven has built on its strong higher education sector by attracting biotech and IT companies.

---

4. We need to do more to celebrate the success of thriving and growing businesses, especially in deprived areas. We want to recognise those whose success contributes to wider prosperity, and challenge the widespread misconception that inner-city, low-income communities are economic "no-go" areas. Inner-city locations can offer real opportunities to business, such as strategic location near major transport hubs, a diverse and available pool of labour and substantial purchasing power. We will:

- sponsor, with the private sector, **the Inner City 25**, which will showcase some of the fastest growing unquoted companies in our most under-invested inner-city areas. This project will demonstrate in a very powerful way that inner-city locations can offer real opportunities for business growth, drawing on United States experience with the Inner City 100, published by Inc magazine in association with the Initiative for a Competitive Inner City.

5. We also want to avoid unnecessary regulatory and financial burdens on small businesses. We are:

- taking forward many of the recommendations of the Better Regulation Task Force's report of April this year about **helping small businesses cope with compliance**. The new Cabinet Office guide to Regulatory Impact Assessment draws attention to how the SBS will help departments to "think small first" and produce regulations which are less burdensome to small business.

- **consulting on reducing business rates for small businesses**. A scheme benefiting all small businesses in England was proposed in the 1998 White Paper *Modern Local Government: In Touch with the People*. Consultation is taking place on this in the Green Paper *Modernising Local Government Finance* published in September 2000. The Green Paper invites views on whether anything more is needed in deprived areas to help small retailers.

continued

Encouraging enterprise in young people

6.   To ensure prosperity in the future we must instil an understanding of business and enterprise in young people. We are encouraging enterprise in young people through:

- including **enterprise education in the National Curriculum**, started in September 2000;

- this year increasing **funding for enterprise programmes in schools**, such as Young Enterprise;

- supporting **Enterprise Insight**, the business-led national enterprise campaign which is focused primarily on engaging young people;

- initiatives which encourage **links between industry and people in higher education**, such as Graduate Apprenticeships and STEP which give undergraduates experience in the work place, and the Higher Education Innovation Fund;

- **Science Enterprise Centres** to teach business and entrepreneurial skills to science, engineering and technology graduates;

- **New Entrepreneur Scholarships**, which will equip young people from deprived areas with the skills needed to start a business. Three pilot projects have begun in Manchester, Greenwich and Plymouth.

Stimulating innovation

7.   We want to encourage the cross-fertilisation of ideas through alliances and partnerships which can stimulate innovative enterprise. We are capitalising on the excellence of the UK research base by encouraging links between local businesses and Higher Education Institutions (HEIs) – over 90% of which are in towns and cities. HEIs have a critical role to play in economic regeneration by providing graduates with the skills businesses need, enabling knowledge exploitation and spin-out companies. HEIs are also key employers and consumers in urban areas. Schemes which encourage transfer of knowledge and best practice include:

- the **University Challenge Fund**, supported by the Wellcome Trust and Gatsby Foundation, which provides seed capital for universities to turn research into successful businesses.

Enterprise and young people: a Bolton example

A project to nurture a culture of enterprise and innovation within the community of 14-19 year olds is being developed in the North West at Mount St Joseph's School Bolton, an inner urban area where there is considerable social deprivation.

It will create a dynamic environment to nurture potential for innovation, embracing technology in its widest sense, driven by learning and 'system thinking' – using as well as acquiring knowledge. The programme could ultimately provide a junior business incubation unit.

Young people will have access to information, manufacturing aids and communication links that could take them into any area (even the board room) of participating companies. They will receive expert mentoring from university lecturers, teachers, parents and industrialists, and have guardians drawn from academic, manufacturing and legal disciplines. The concept could well be considered for earlier action in primary school.

The project involves the community and aims to build, equip and support an innovation centre to stimulate enterprise, entrepreneurialism and creative thinking at a very early age.

---

continued

5

- The Higher Education Reach Out to Business and the Community Fund, which will be incorporated into the new **Higher Education Innovation Fund** as announced in the Science and Innovation White Paper. This new fund worth £140m over three years will further increase the capability of higher education to respond to the needs of business and the wider community. This will include helping to establish new subsidiary and spin-out companies, encourage knowledge exchange and skills development, provide one-stop shops for businesses seeking support from higher education and increase the number of university courses designed for industry.

- **Faraday Partnerships**, linking universities and independent research organisations with business and finance, to develop new products and processes. The Government is doubling the number of new starts for these partnerships so that by 2002 we will have a network of 24 across the UK.

- **LINK**, which provides matched funding to promote partnership in pre-competitive research between industry and universities.

- **Research and Development Tax Credit** for corporate small and medium enterprises. The Government has introduced, from April 2000, an increase in tax relief on research and development spending from 100% to 150%.

- **Manufacturing Centres of Excellence** which will be able to provide hands on advice and assistance on technology and manufacturing best practice.

Clusters

8.   We want to support innovation, competitiveness, and economic development within the regions. One way of doing this is to encourage support for clusters. Clusters are geographic concentrations of interconnected companies, specialist suppliers, service providers, firms in related industries, and associated institutions in particular fields that compete but also co-operate. The expertise available in an HEI is often an important element of a cluster. While clusters are not solely urban, many are located in towns and cities.

9.   Business incubators and managed workspace can play a key role in both cluster development and economic regeneration more generally. Business incubators typically provide a structured environment to assist young companies through provision of premises, advice and access to seedcorn funding, allowing the entrepreneur to concentrate their effort on developing their business idea. Research shows that participation in a business incubation programme significantly enhances the survival rate of new businesses.

A business incubator tailored to women's needs: The Wellpark Enterprise Centre

The Wellpark Enterprise Centre in Glasgow is an extremely successful business incubator tailored specifically to women's needs. As well as operating 20 managed workspace, the centre runs a whole range of highly innovative programmes (including microcredit schemes, business training, pre-start-up and start-up grants and outreach work) and has achieved excellent results in helping women start up and run successful businesses.

Incubators offer flexible provision and immediate access to peer groups, networks and mentoring – all of which are crucial in supporting women.

---

10.   Planning for business creation in a cluster is important. *Planning Policy Guidance Note 12* (PPG12) requires local authorities to set out in Development Plans appropriate land use policies in support of cluster development and growth. PPG11 makes clear that regional planning bodies should work with RDAs to plan proactively to facilitate the establishment and expansion of clusters and that development plans should allow for business incubator units to be at the heart of clusters.

continued

11. In order to facilitate the development of clusters, and to build on existing strengths and activities in the regions, we have announced a **new Regional Innovation Fund** which will be distributed by the RDAs to support projects which further the objectives set out in Regional Strategies. This will complement the existing Innovative Clusters Fund and raise the available funding to £50m a year. The new fund will:

- support innovative sectoral/geographical networks, including clusters;

- promote property/facility options for businesses starting up;

- provide business incubator facilities;

- promote access to and application of new technologies by small and medium-sized enterprises;

- establish innovation centres and other centres of excellence in response to business needs; and

- develop economic observatories – virtual centres to collect and disseminate information on the economic status of the region and its strengths and weaknesses – allowing the RDA, its partners and companies in the region to respond quickly and appropriately to new developments.

South East England Development Agency: supporting enterprise and innovation through the Enterprise Hubs Programme

The South East has the highest business start up rate in Britain but also the highest rate of failure. The objective of Enterprise Hubs is to promote economic growth, by creating the right conditions for local businesses to thrive and breaking down barriers to growth. This includes improving entrepreneurial access to technology, research and innovation; improving access to investment; and supporting growth of jobs in the knowledge economy.

SEEDA aims to create a regional network of 25-30 Enterprise Hubs over the next 5 years, providing centres of excellence for each of the region's key clusters.

Each hub will be led by a local community of entrepreneurs and run by a Hub Director. Each will provide: incubator space for new businesses, strong links with venture capitalists, an affiliated university research department or other commercial research facility, and agreed strategies with the Small Business Service and Learning and Skills Council at local level.

A key element is provision of incubator space to address an identified shortage. SEEDA is co-ordinating a programme for the construction of incubator units across the South East, with investment from the Innovative Clusters Fund providing pump priming to make rapid progress.

The Enterprise Hubs programme has already doubled the amount of quality incubator space under construction in the region to 500,000 sq ft. SEEDA expect the programme to achieve, within the next five years: at least 600 more business start-ups a year across the South East; 25% improvement on business start-ups surviving after two years; £300m new investment in South East companies; and 10,000 companies reporting improvements to performance as a direct result of enterprise hubs.

continued

5

Information and communications technology

12. The information and communications revolution is one of the biggest challenges and opportunities facing our economy today. It has changed forever the way we do business and communicate with one another. To be successful businesses in cities and towns need to embrace e-business and e-commerce and seize the opportunities they present.

13. Our aim is to make the UK one of the world's leading knowledge economies by creating the right environment for e-commerce to thrive, helping businesses get online and giving everyone who wants it access to the internet by 2005. We have already taken a number of steps to do this including:

- passing the **Electronic Communications Act 2000** which ensures that electronic signatures are legally admissible as evidence in court in the same way as hand-written signatures; and

- setting up **TrustUK**, a Government-backed industry scheme to hallmark codes of practice for e-commerce to ensure they protect consumers.

14. Already 1.7 million small and medium sized enterprises are on line – 81% of all UK businesses. This has smashed the UK's target which was to get 1.5 million businesses online by 2002. But there is more to do:

- The Government recently launched **UK online** in partnership with industry, voluntary organisations, trades unions and consumer groups, supported by over £2 billion. The key elements of UK online are:

  - **UK online for business** – £15m of extra funding over 2 years, in addition to the £10m for 2001/02 announced in this year's budget – to expand the network of 103 UK online for Business Centres offering accessible, independent and jargon-free IT advice to businesses. These are being integrated into the Small Business Service in England and their equivalents in the rest of the UK;

  - **UK online centres** – By the end of 2002 there will also be 6,000 government-funded UK Online centres. These will provide people with access to new technologies and help them develop the skills to use them. All public libraries will be on-line, and staff will be trained to help people make the most of the services. UK Online centres will be sited wherever best suits the needs of local people: community centres, schools, churches or even converted buses;

  - **ukonline.gov.uk** – going live later this year to provide a single online point of entry to government information and services.

15. We are also looking to the **next wave of high-speed communications technologies** for which services are starting to become available, to provide the means for businesses of all sizes to compete. We will continue to promote competition, through measures such as local loop unbundling, to ensure that these technologies are rolled out quickly to as much of the country as possible.

16. We recognise that the market, left to itself, may not provide a complete solution. We will therefore work through the development agencies in the regions, Northern Ireland, Scotland, and Wales to develop effective strategies for the comprehensive provision of **higher bandwidth services**, taking full advantage of opportunities for the development of public-private partnerships supported, for example, by EU funding.

17. We will also keep under review the case for extending the existing universal service obligation for basic telephony to cover broadband, although we consider that the broadband market is insufficiently developed at present to justify extending the obligation.

continued

e-commerce brings business success to Wigan sports clothing company

Optimum Design, established in 1991, specialises in the design, development and sale of protective sports clothing, selling its products wholesale via 10 agents around the UK and over 1000 independent sports retailers in Europe. In 1998, Optimum Design was encouraged, after speaking to the local UK online for business adviser, to enter the world of e-commerce – initially setting up a basic three page website; then developing a business-to-business strategy to ensure a more streamlined supply chain, and launching (with help from a local design company) a 50 page secure ordering site to complement the company's mail order/direct mail operation. The website has increased brand awareness, kept customers aware of new products and news, and extended sales to new areas. The company now attracts 14,000 website hits per week, and this is reflected in company turnover which has increased from £110,000 in 1993 to £730,000 in 1999. Optimium Design's next step is to address language barriers reflecting the increasing number of sales abroad, and the website will soon become a fully integrated language site.

Key enterprise and innovation PSA targets[1]

- Improve UK competitiveness by narrowing the productivity gap with US, France, Germany and Japan over the economic cycle (HMT/DTI)

- Help build an enterprise society in which small firms of all kinds thrive and achieve their potential, with an increase in the number of people considering going into business, an improvement in the overall productivity of small firms, and more enterprise in disadvantaged communities. (DTI)

- Make and keep the UK the best place in the world to trade electronically, as measured by the cost of Internet access and the extent of business-to-business and business-to-consumer transactions carried out over e-commerce networks. (DTI)

- Improve the economic performance of all regions measured by trend in growth of each region's GDP per capita. (DTI/DETR)

- Increase the level of exploitation of technological knowledge derived from the science and engineering base, as demonstrated by a significant rise in the proportion of innovating businesses citing such sources. (DTI)

[1] Extracted from Objectives and Performance Targets published following Spending Review 2000.

5

ACTION TO CREATE AND SHARE PROSPERITY
2. Encouraging increased investment

1. Investment in enterprise is essential in order to deliver jobs and opportunity for all. Investment is needed to help enterprises across all sectors develop their full potential. The box below illustrates this through the example of the tourism sector which plays a significant role in contributing to the UK economy and providing employment opportunities.

2. At regional level, we have given RDAs responsibility for marketing their region as a business location for **overseas inward investment**, working in partnership with Invest-UK, the Government's national inward investment agency. RDAs have a pivotal role in bringing together the different players in their region for the promotion of inward investment – both in attracting new projects, and helping to sustain and add value to existing investor development.

Investing in enterprise: Tourism

In 2000, tourists – including 26 million overseas visitors – will contribute over £64 billion to the UK economy and support 1.8 million jobs. The same things that make cities and towns interesting places for us are also important to them – our heritage and culture and attractions like entertainment, restaurants, bars and shops.

Most tourism (72% in England) takes place in urban areas but it is unevenly spread. We need to manage tourism in popular destinations to ensure that their success is not eventually degraded through over use, develop new destinations as a way of boosting the economy and regeneration, and revive destinations which have seen a decline in popularity.

To do this the Government has:

- created the English Tourism Council (ETC) to provide strategic leadership to the industry and to help develop more sustainable forms of tourism;

- boosted the British Tourist Authority's funding in 2001/02 to £37m to promote Britain overseas and to target particular markets like film, sports and cultural tourism;

- supported the Business Tourism Partnership to develop the convention, exhibition and travel incentives markets particularly in areas which don't normally benefit from leisure and tourism;

- Asked the ETC to prepare a national strategy for revitalising England's seaside resorts and encouraged the availability of funding for resort based regeneration from sources like the National Lottery and Europe.

There are already major tourism successes springing up in urban locations which never previously attracted visitors or which have declined in popularity in recent years. The new Tate Modern, the Lowry centre in Salford, Birmingham's canalside development, the redevelopment of Nottingham's historic lace market and the revival of Brighton all offer good examples from which we can learn.

The BA London Eye is one of many successful tourist attractions that have recently opened around the country (Photograph courtesy of BA).

continued

Overseas inward investment: a Liverpool example

Recently Bertelsmann from Germany have announced the setting up of a customer services and technical support centre in Liverpool city centre. The project will create 349 jobs, with a total fixed investment of over £2.2m. Bertelsmann is the world's third largest (and Europe's largest) media production and distribution company.

This project involved the North West Development Agency, working with the Government Office for the North West, Liverpool City Council (and Liverpool Vision – the regeneration company), the Merseyside TEC, as well as Invest-UK.

3. At the level of individual businesses, many enterprises in our least well-off communities have difficulty in accessing support, advice and finance. The Bank of England is about to publish the first in a series of annual reports on access to finance for businesses in deprived areas. The report will draw on evidence from an extensive series of regional visits undertaken by the Bank and on the Banks' own data. It will cover a range of potential sources of finance, including banks and community finance initiatives. In addition the Government has:

- Encouraged availability of **risk finance** through a series of programmes which support:

  – the small firms loan guarantee scheme

  – at least one venture capital fund in each of the English regions, providing small-scale equity and drawing in local expertise from the RDAs and others. This will be implemented early in 2001 subject to State Aid clearance

  – the UK high technology fund to support early stage high technology businesses.

- In Budget 2000, the Chancellor of the Exchequer announced a new **target umbrella fund** to build on the regional venture capital funds and others. The Government has committed £100m to the fund which will eventually form a pot of £1 billion to support regional, local and sub-local enterprises, focusing on better access to early stage finance for small firms.

- As explained in the section above on encouraging enterprise across society, we have created a new £30m **Phoenix Fund** to invest over three years in promoting better access to business support and finance.

4. The UK will receive well over **£10 billion from the EU structural funds** for the period 2000 to 2006 – around £1.5 billion a year. European structural funding can support a variety of activities to improve economic performance, including support for small businesses, community economic development, environmental enhancement and vocational training. Urban areas are one of the priorities for the structural funds and very significant amounts will go to urban areas under the main Objective 1, 2 and 3 programmes. There is also an EU Community Initiative specifically for urban communities, worth some £75m to the UK. This will be targeted at a small number of projects to help deprived urban areas in each part of the UK.

continued

5

European funds to support economic and social restructuring: strategic regeneration in Wolverhampton

Wolverhampton has been working hard to renew its sense of purpose and generate new jobs following the decline of manufacturing and the steel industry. Europe has played a major role in supporting and enabling change.

Following an extensive audit and consultation of the local community and businesses, a detailed people-oriented urban regeneration action programme was drawn up and European funding was targeted at regenerating two main areas of the town:

- the Cultural Quarter: the Chubb building where locks and safes were once manufactured, now houses a number of growing multimedia small and medium enterprises and is the focal point of the quarter. Schemes to improve the art gallery, the Grand Theatre and the University's Arena Theatre, combined with training and business support initiatives, are promoting economic opportunities in the cultural and media sector;

- the Urban Village project – this is a community based approach to improving living conditions in the All Saints area, one of the most deprived in the region, through setting up community businesses, supporting the most disadvantaged groups and fostering cultural and media businesses.

The total project budget was £19m, including £5.8m EU contribution. Between 1993 and 1998 Wolverhampton's regeneration programme generated 1500 jobs and 75 SMEs, including 32 cultural businesses.

5. We shall do more:

The **Social Investment Task Force**, led by leading venture capitalist Ronald Cohen of Apax Partners & Co, reported to the Chancellor in October. Its report, *Enterprising Communities: Wealth Beyond Welfare*, recommended a five-point programme of action aimed at stimulating enterprise, investment and wealth creation in under-invested communities.

6. The report's main recommendations are:

- a new Community Investment Tax Credit to encourage private investment in both not-for-profit and profit-seeking enterprises in under-invested communities;

- a new Community Development Venture Fund – a matched funding partnership between Government on the one hand and the venture capital industry, entrepreneurs, institutional investors and banks on the other;

- disclosure by individual banks of their funding activities to businesses in under-invested communities and the creation of a rating system to reward excellent performance. The Taskforce believes this should if possible be done on a voluntary basis, but if not, then legislation should require disclosure;

- greater latitude and encouragement for charitable trusts and foundations to invest in community development initiatives; and

- support for Community Development Financial Institutions, which provide finance and business support to enterprises just outside the margin of conventional finance; and the appointment of a high ranking champion for community development finance, with strong links to Government.

7. The Government welcomes this innovative report and endorses its central conclusion that enterprise and wealth creation are vital to building sustainable communities. The Government is already supporting the growth of community development finance for businesses in under-invested areas. In response to the Cohen report, the Government will now do more:

- The Government believes that a tax incentive for community investment could prove effective in helping to bring more investment and expertise to the economic renewal of disadvantaged communities. The Government will consult widely on the proposal for a Community Investment Tax Credit, with a view to taking it forward as early as possible.

- The Government will work closely with the venture capital industry and others on setting up the first Community Development Venture Fund.

- The Government attaches great importance to making financial services available to all. To provide greter transparency, the Government will encourage banks to disclose their individual lending activities to businesses in under-invested areas. The Government will look at what obligations should be laid on banks in the context of the overall requirements being asked of them, for example in relation to Universal Banking Services.

- The Government believes that the Taskforce has set out very clearly the challenges that lie in front of the community development finance sector in the UK, if it is to achieve it's potential. It must be a matter for the sector to respond to these challenges, but the Government will continue to play an active role in support, for example through assistance with training. The Government also recognises that there may be a role for an informal "champion" and will consider how to take this suggestion forward.

Key investment PSA targets[2]

- Maintain the UK as the prime location in the EU for foreign direct investment. (DTI/FCO)

- Improve the economic performance of all regions measured by trend in growth of each region's GDP per capita. (DTI/DETR)

---

[2] Extracted from Objectives and Performance Targets published following Spending Review 2000.

5

ACTION TO CREATE AND SHARE PROSPERITY
3. Providing employment opportunities for all

1. Human capital is one of the most important factors to a company in deciding where to locate. But education and training have in the past often failed to match the ability of the workforce to the needs of the economy. Creating a skilled and flexible labour force in cities and towns is vital if we are to:

- respond and adapt to the changing needs of an increasingly sophisticated economy;

- encourage companies to come to, and remain in, cities and towns; and

- maximise people's employment opportunities.

Equipping people with skills

2. We must equip people with the skills they need for the jobs of the future and address the fact that high rates of unemployment often sit alongside skills shortages. We are already putting many of the important building blocks in place.
We are:

- improving **school education** to give people the basic literacy, numeracy and other skills they need to play their part in a modern competitive economy. (See Chapter 6);

- aiming to ensure that the **participation and achievement of pupils from ethnic minorities** matches that of the population as a whole. We are taking action to raise the educational achievement of ethnic minority children as an integral element of standards, inclusion and equal opportunities agendas. In 2001/02 the Ethnic Minority Achievement Grant Programme will support some £153.5m of local spending to raise the achievement of ethnic minority pupils – an increase of £6m over the current year. There are encouraging signs that Government initiatives are beginning to bear fruit: the recently published Key Stage 2 test results show that inner city LEAs with high ethnic minority populations are among the most improved in the country.

- developing a workforce with the advanced skills necessary to meet the needs of high-tech, competitive and mobile employers. We are setting a target for fifty percent of young people to benefit from **higher education** by the time they reach the age of 30, and are widening participation in further education to engage those who have traditionally not taken advantage of learning opportunities;

- strengthening **efforts to increase young people's skills**, by measures such as

  – giving 16-17 year old employees the right to reasonable paid time off to pursue approved qualifications up to level 2;

  – developing technician, supervisory and craft-level skills among 16-24 year olds through the Advanced Modern Apprenticeship;

- promoting a **culture of lifelong learning** through drawing more and different groups of people into further education and pioneering new, alternative learning opportunities to attract and motivate adults, especially in deprived neighbourhoods – such as:

  – a rise of £150m in funds for adult basic skills, targeted at increasing basic adult numeracy, literacy and computer skills.

  – the £20m Adult and Community Learning Fund for projects including basic and study support skills training for disadvantaged parents;

- improving access and availability of relevant high quality learning through the new on-line **University for Industry** also known as learndirect. With a £118m fund over two years, this learning network is aimed at both individuals and businesses to improve the nation's competitiveness by raising people's skills and employability. It will stimulate demand for lifelong learning among adults, and small and medium size employers by providing advice for up to 2.5 million people a year by 2002, and stimulate demand for up to 1 million courses and learning packages a year by 2003.

continued

3. These actions will have a long-term impact on the ability of our workforce to meet the challenges of the future. In recognition of the importance of the challenge we are now:

- setting out to improve the quality and relevance of post-16 education and training for individuals, employers and communities through the new national **Learning and Skills Council**. This will bring together funding for education and training under a single organisation, to ensure a coherent and responsive approach to improving the quality of learning for the benefit of learners and employers alike. A key priority will be to engage more low-skilled people from deprived neighbourhoods through a diverse range of range of local, community-based learning opportunities. It will use around £6 billion a year (including school sixth form funding) to improve skills for almost 6 million learners;

- offering individuals a way to invest in their learning alongside the government and other stakeholders such as employers through **Individual Learning Accounts**. We have set a target of opening 500,000 Individual Learning Accounts by April 2001;

- driving up quality in colleges by increasing the **Further Education Standards Fund** to £160m in 2001/02;

Bridging the Gap

"Bridging the Gap" is a project aimed at regenerating the area around the Evelyn Estate in Deptford, South London, by providing a people-related approach to deliver education, training, and employment opportunities, creating youth employment and new business opportunities, improving community safety and building social cohesion.

The Evelyn Estate is straddled by the railway viaduct which runs from Greenwich to London Bridge. It contains hundreds of arches, some of which were in gainful use, but many of which were empty. The project, backed by some £5m of public money and £3m of private funding over four years, has three main capital elements:

- the derelict Windsor Castle pub in Deptford High Street has been gutted, refitted and turned into a Youth Drop-in centre, providing training and counselling.

- the Arches project, opened in November 1998 by Nick Raynsford, has turned railway arches into a cafe and shop where vocational training in retailing and catering is given, as well while providing new facilities for local people.

- The Parkside Enterprise Centre is a business support and advice centre for business wanting to set up in and around the arches.

As a result of Bridging the Gap, 48 jobs have been created; 197 individuals have become involved in voluntary work; 68 voluntary organisations have been supported; over 10,000 young people have benefited from projects to promote personal and social development and 42 new businesses have started up.

(Photographs: Richard Townshend)

continued

- piloting **Education Maintenance Allowances** to test whether a financial incentive to young people from low-income families will encourage more to stay on and achieve in learning beyond 16. We will set up additional pilots from 2000/01;

- encouraging stronger and more systematic **links between higher education and business** to ensure that we have a workforce with the skills to meet the needs of employers in the knowledge-based and global economy. The new Foundation Degrees and Graduate Apprenticeships will both play an important role in this; and

Matching skills provision to market needs: South East Village

The South East Regional Development Agency, SEEDA, has brought together and co-located 11 partners from across the learning and skills spectrum –

- five National Training Organisations (covering construction; engineering and marine; electronics and software services; agriculture and horticulture; and broadcasting, film and video);

- University for Industry;

- Skills Insight (a joint venture of the eight Business Links and SEEDA to research skills needs);

- Higher Education South East (representing the region's 25 universities);

- the Association of South East Colleges of Further Education (representing 71 Further Education Colleges);

- RAISE (the regional co-ordinating body for the voluntary sector); and

- the Further Education Development Agency.

The objective is to adopt a holistic approach to skills needs by linking market needs to educational providers, so as to anticipate and react to skills needs.

- providing for each RDA to develop a tailor-made **Regional Skills Strategy** and a detailed Regional Skills Action Plan, so that training will meet the needs of both employers and individuals. The Government has provided an additional £10m in 2000/01 for Regional Skills Development Funds, and announced a further £8.5m for 2001/02.

Employment opportunities for all

4. Our vision for cities and towns includes residents sharing in higher living standards through employment. This means people without a job need to be willing to take advantage of the employment opportunities out there; and employers need to be willing to consider the widest range of people for the jobs on offer.

5. The Government's welfare to work policy aims to help people not in employment, particularly those on welfare, into work so all can share in higher living standards and greater job opportunities. Employment has increased by over 1 million since spring 1997. We have:

- helped into work well over 244,000 young people and 70,000 long-term unemployed people, among others, on the **New Deal programmes** for 18-24 year olds, the long term unemployed, the over 50s, lone parents, partners of unemployed people and disabled people – which concentrate support on those who find it most difficult to obtain work and improve their prospects of remaining in sustained employment. Personal Advisers consider with Participants how to break down barriers to employment through programmes such as improving basic skills and understanding the qualities that employers are looking for, training opportunities, in-work benefits and where appropriate, information on local childcare provision;

continued

- found new solutions to help people find and stay in work in areas of considerable labour market disadvantage, by creating **15 Employment Zones** which have helped over 1,000 long-term unemployed people into work. At their heart is the Personal Job Account, a key innovation, which gives the participant and their personal adviser more control over funds from a range of sources.

The New Deal: helping people back into employment
(Photograph: Richard Townshend)

- amongst other measures to promote equal opportunities, we have set targets – not quotas – for the **representation of women, ethnic minorities and disabled people** in the Senior Civil Service, for which many of the posts are located in urban areas. Targets have also been set for the recruitment, retention and promotion of ethnic minorities in the police, fire, probation and prison services in line with our view that public authorities should aim to be representative of the communities that they serve.

6. We have also **reformed taxes and benefits** to ensure that work pays more than welfare and to overcome specific barriers to work. For many people, especially those who have been out of work for long periods, the transition back into work can be a difficult period. Some groups require additional support – in particular, families with children can be constrained by the costs and availability of childcare.

We have:

- introduced the Working Families' Tax Credit;

- reformed National Insurance contributions;

- introduced the 10p starting rate of income tax and a lower basic rate of income tax at 22p;

- developed our National Childcare Strategy to help ensure affordable, high quality childcare by creating more childcare places for 1.6 million children by 2004, and setting up a system to register and inspect childcare providers; and

- underpinned these reforms by the National Minimum Wage.

7. We want to ease the transition from welfare to work. To help with this, Budget 2000 announced:

- a £100 job grant to help people make the transition from welfare to work;

- extended payments of Income Support for Mortgage Interest when moving into work, to match the housing benefit run-on already available;

- simplified rules for applying for these payments to increase take-up; and

- a new childcare tax credit.

8. Government policies are designed to encourage employers to consider the widest range of people for the jobs on offer – including the long-term unemployed, the economically inactive, people with disabilities, people from ethnic minorities and older people. We shall now do more to help people who feel excluded from the job market, particularly in the areas that need the most help. We will:

- actively support people in becoming more independent, on the basis of work for those who can and security for those who cannot, through a new **Working Age Agency** which we will launch in Summer 2001. It will have a clear focus on work, providing a proactive and responsive service to employers, helping people to find jobs and helping employers to fill their vacancies with the right people;

- offer people a single point of access for work-focused support and help with benefit queries for all benefits claimants of working age, called **"ONE"**. We will keep running this in 12 pilot areas over the next couple of years to test it comprehensively;

continued

- set up **40 new Action Teams for Jobs**, using a £45.5m fund, into selected areas with primarily low employment rates, high unemployment rates or a high proportion of disadvantaged ethnic minority groups. They will help to overcome the individual barriers preventing jobless people filling nearby vacancies;

- further enhance a number of New Deal programmes in 2001; and

- continue to combat unjustified discrimination in the workplace. We welcome the **EU Framework Directive on equal treatment at work**, and will be consulting on proposals for legislation to implement it.

Bolton Ethnic Minority Forum – tackling barriers to employment

In the run up to New Deal for 18-24 year olds, the district team in Bolton organised a focus group with potential clients and organisations to ensure that the New Deal Partnership would have adequate representation of people who were able to understand fully the needs of people from ethnic minority backgrounds and monitor its effectiveness as New Deal Develops. The Group looked at the particular barriers young people from an ethnic minority background face when trying to access employment, education and training. The meeting also provided the opportunity to detail the kind of provision these clients felt they needed. The delegates recognised that the partnership being formed was lacking an adequate representation of people who understood the needs of the target group. As result of the meetings, an Ethnic Minority Forum was set up comprising 15 organisations and has since opened an effective channel of communications between local minority ethnic communities, the Employment Service and key local partners.

Key PSA targets[3]

- By 2004, increase by 3% the numbers of 19 year olds achieving a qualification equivalent to National Vocational Qualification level 2 compared to 2002. (DfEE)

- In Higher Education, while maintaining standards:

  – Increase participation towards 50% of those aged 18 – 30 by the end of the decade;

  – Make significant year on year progress towards fair access, as measured by the Funding Council benchmarks; and

  – Bear down on rates of non-completion (DfEE).

- Reduce the number of adults who have literacy or numeracy problems by 750,000 by 2004 (DfEE).

- Over the 3 years to 2004, increase the employment rates of disadvantaged areas and groups, taking account of the economic cycle – women, people with disabilities, lone parents, ethnic minorities and the over 50s, the 30 local authority districts with the poorest initial labour market position – and reduce the difference between their employment rates and the overall rate (DfEE).

- Make substantial progress towards eradicating child poverty by reducing the number of children in poverty by at least a quarter by 2004 (HMT/DSS).

- Reduce the number of children in households with no-one in work over the 3 years to 2004 (DfEE).

---

[3] Extracted from *Objectives and Performance Targets* published following Spending Review 2000.

ACTION TO CREATE AND SHARE PROSPERITY
4. Providing an efficient, reliable and safe transport system

1. Modern, efficient transport services:

- are essential to the effective functioning of local economies, communities and neighbourhoods, and provide vital links to national and international markets;

- have a direct effect on the quality of people's daily lives, and on their access to jobs, services and leisure opportunities; and

- have a major part to play in making our towns and cities more attractive places in which to live and work.

2. *Transport 2010 – The 10 Year Plan*, published in July 2000, sets out how we will meet the challenge of modernising and improving transport through a major programme of investment. It will deliver a step change in the quality of transport provision. The Plan sets out a long-term strategy that has amongst its key objectives contributing to the renaissance of towns and cities, reducing social exclusion and promoting business competitiveness and economic development.

3. For towns and cities outside London the new statutory Local Transport Plans (LTPs) will be the main means of delivering the new investment. LTPs should be developed as part of the local vision for each area, in conjunction with local planning and economic development strategies. They should be developed in an inclusive and participative way, in full consultation with local communities and business. The new Transport Bill will also give local authorities powers to set up congestion charging schemes or workplace parking levies in their areas in order to tackle local transport problems.

4. Funding for LTPs outside London will double in the first year of the 10 Year Plan, with further sustained increases thereafter. Total spending on local transport over the Plan period will be £59 billion, with a further £25 billion for much-needed transport improvements in London. Cities and towns will also benefit from the £60 billion that will be spent on improving national railways and the £21 billion to be spent on strategic roads.

5. Local authorities and the Mayor of London will be responsible for setting their own priorities. But for people in towns and cities, these levels of funding are expected to deliver by 2010:

- new infrastructure to promote economic development in regeneration areas including up to 25 new light rail or tram lines in major cities;

- major bus infrastructure schemes (including guided bus projects) in many cities and towns;

- much higher quality bus services;

- up to 100 new park and ride schemes;

- more frequent and reliable rail services, with modern trains and better stations;

- up to 100 major road improvement schemes including bypasses and junction improvements to improve safety and ease congestion;

- elimination of the substantial road maintenance backlog;

- a major expansion in local traffic management schemes, safer routes for cycling and walking, and local environmental improvements in towns and cities across the country;

- increased capacity and improved services on the London Underground; and

- new East-West and orbital rail links in London.

6. This new programme of investment, together with better linkages between development planning, regeneration policies and transport provision will make cities and towns function better. The 10 Year Plan for transport will play a significant role in making our towns and cities better places in which to live, work and do business by delivering:

- less congested, safer and better maintained roads;

- reduced impacts from traffic and a better quality urban environment (see also Chapter 4);

continued

- a step change in the quality of public transport services in our larger urban areas;

- better access to town centres, jobs and services, including from deprived areas;

- more efficient freight distribution; and

- better access to ports and airports and a more integrated transport system.

7. Children, older people, people with disabilities and people in households with lower incomes are all more reliant on public transport. 60% of the poorest 20% of households have no car. Lack of efficient, affordable public transport services therefore has a disproportionate effect on these groups, contributing to deprivation and social exclusion.

Low floor buses provide better access for mobility impaired people.

8. Measures aimed particularly at increasing access for these groups include:

- a new Urban Bus Challenge Fund to provide improved links to deprived areas or isolated estates;

- statutory concessionary fare schemes for all pensioners and disabled people, entitling them to free bus passes giving at least half-fare reductions;

- fare reductions for young people entering employment through the New Deal, and discounts for those remaining in education beyond 16;

- the extension of the fuel duty rebate to some forms of community transport;

- initiatives, such as the Secure Stations Scheme, to improve personal security for all at stations, in car parks and on public transport;

- new requirements to ensure that the needs of disabled people are factored into all new transport provision; and

- a new Gender Audit checklist which offers transport operators and other providers a framework for checking that services within their responsibility take adequate account of the different needs of their customers.

Key transport PSA targets[4]

- Reduce road congestion in large urban areas below current levels by 2010 by promoting integrated transport solutions and investing in public transport and the road network.

- Increase bus use from 2000 levels by 10% by 2010, while improving punctuality and reliability.

- Double light rail use from 2000 levels by 2010.

- Reduce the number of people killed or seriously injured in GB in road accidents by 40% by 2010 and the number of children killed or seriously injured by 50% compared with the average for 1994-98.

- Increase rail use in Great Britain by 50% between 2000 and 2010, while improving punctuality and reliability.

- Cut journey times on London Underground by increasing capacity and reducing delays.

[4] Extracted from Objectives and Performance Targets published following Spending Review 2000.

Quality services and opportunities for all

The Government's aim is for good public services to attract and keep people and businesses in towns and cities and to give everyone the opportunity to realise their full potential.

Contents

Introduction

6.1 The majority of people living in urban areas enjoy good services, safe surroundings and opportunities to enjoy culture, leisure and sport.

6.2 Others do not. In some areas there are poor quality services and people live in fear of crime. This denies opportunities to those living in those communities and contributes to people's decisions to move out in search of a better quality of life

6.3 Good services are also important if we are to create economically successful cities and towns. Business location decisions are influenced by factors such as the quality of the education system and the availability of good health care. And lack of good housing or high crime rates can also act as a deterrent to businesses looking to locate in urban areas. Conversely, top class cultural, sporting or exhibition venues, for example, add to the attractiveness of cities as places to do business or as tourism destinations. These facilities often serve a wider area than the town or city concerned – the concert halls in Birmingham or Manchester, for example, are regional if not national venues.

6.4 We are at the start of a period of major investment in the improvement of our public services. The investment will be linked with change in the way public services are delivered, with clear targets setting out what is expected of services, effective partnership working arrangements for providing public services and active community involvement. Quality services are an essential part of the fabric of a civilised society. They will make towns and cities better places for all.

Current position

6.5   The last century saw marked improvements in the quality of life of most people, associated with better housing, a better environment and increased prosperity. Over 80% of householders in urban[1] areas in England say that they are very or fairly satisfied with the area they live in and the great majority of people in England are satisfied with the way councils run local services.

6.6   But where there are problems, such as poor health, fear of crime, actual crime and poor educational performance, they impact more on urban areas. On average, those living in our larger cities and conurbations fall behind the rest of the country on a number of key indices.

People living in conurbations:

- achieve **lower educational results**[2]: 10.9% of pupils aged 15 achieve no or only low grade GCSEs, compared with 6.4% across England

- have a **lower employment rate**[3]: 70.6% compared with 74.3% in the UK as a whole

- have more children living in **poverty**[4]: 37.6% of children live in households dependent on income support, compared with 25.7% across England

- are generally **less healthy** and have a higher probability of dying[5]: every year there are up to 3900 more deaths in our main cities than should be expected given the mortality rate for the UK

- are 19% more likely to experience violent **crime**, 46% more likely to experience burglary and 35% more likely to experience vehicle related theft[6].

Delivering quality services for all

6.7   The Government is determined to improve public services for everyone. We have:

- put in place a public sector modernisation programme to deliver efficient, high-quality public services which meet the needs of citizens not service providers;

- set challenging targets to ensure the minimum quality of service is delivered in all areas;

- introduced the new 'Best Value' regime for local government, together with Local Public Service Agreement targets, so that councils will have to seek continually to improve the quality and efficiency of what they provide; and

- announced substantially increased resources for all the main public services in Spending Review 2000.

6.8   We are looking for substantial improvements in all key service areas.

Education

6.9   Securing Britain's economic future demands that pupils achieve much higher standards of education. This is vital to enable people to achieve their potential and get jobs; provide a skilled and flexible labour force; and make young people less likely to become involved in crime or anti-social behaviour. We have made substantial progress in implementing a manifesto for excellence. We intend to build the capacity of communities to help themselves and bring about social cohesion right across the country.

6.10   In particular, our **Excellence in Cities programme** will improve the education of city children and build parents' confidence in the education service, driving up standards in schools in major cities higher and faster by focusing on the needs of individual pupils. The Government is determined that every child should benefit from the rise in standards, and that no particular groups should be excluded or left behind.

---

[1] 'Urban' here includes suburban areas.

[2] Metropolitan areas referred to are cities of Manchester, Liverpool, Sheffield, Newcastle upon Tyne, Birmingham and Leeds. The figure for Inner London is 8.8%. Figures based on 1997 data.

[3] Metropolitan areas referred to are metropolitan counties of Tyne and Wear, Greater Manchester, Merseyside, South Yorkshire, West Yorkshire and the West Midlands. It also includes London. DfEE Spring 2000.

[4] Areas referred to are the main cities as in (2). The figure for Inner London is 49.1%. Based on 1996 data.

[5] This figure refers to all the main cities above together with Inner London. The number of excess deaths in any particular area is the difference between the observed number of deaths in that area and the number that would be expected if the area had the same age specific mortality rates as the UK. The data used is based on combined data for 1991-97.

[6] *British Crime Survey 2000* published October. Comparisons based on inner cities and the national average.

6.11 We are pumping £6 billion a year into **Higher Education Institutions**. They help to regenerate cities, for example, Durham University's new Stockton campus which helped redevelop an industrial wasteland; they provide skilled professionals in, for example, medicine, teaching and community work, to live and work in the city; their staff and students working in the community can make a major contribution to capacity building and raising aspirations; and they provide access to cultural, sports and adult education facilities, giving many communities a gateway into higher education.

Health

6.12 Our aim is a health service designed around the patient that offers people fast and convenient care delivered to a consistently high standard. Services will be available when people require them, tailored to their individual needs.

6.13 We will improve health and reduce inequality by working in partnership with other agencies to tackle the causes of ill health and we will provide increased resources to improve primary care services in deprived areas and the inner cities, where these services are in most need of expansion. **The NHS Plan** contains a fundamental programme of reform to take this forward.

Crime

6.14 The Government is committed to reducing crime. Clear targets have been set and the strategy to achieve them is based on: providing the police with the officers, resources and technological support they need to tackle crime effectively; bringing more offenders to justice; supporting **Crime and Disorder Partnerships** to bring together all the different agencies which can contribute to crime reduction at the local levels; and reflecting in future expenditure plans for education, health and housing the specific contribution they can make to crime reduction.

Housing

6.15 Our aim is to deliver quality and choice across the housing market – tackling the problems of poor condition stock and social exclusion and giving everyone the opportunity of a decent home. We have set ourselves the target of bringing all social housing up to a decent standard within ten years and have set out a range of proposals in the **Green Paper on Housing** to tackle poor quality housing in the private sector.

Waltham Forest Housing Action Trust

Waltham Forest Housing Action Trust is achieving excellent progress towards the holistic regeneration of an area of north-east London. The HAT is now less than two years away from the end of its life but has its successor bodies, O-Regen and the Waltham Forest Community Based Housing Association (CBHA), in place to ensure that the regeneration work already achieved remains sustainable. O-Regen delivers economic and community services while the CBHA manages the HAT estates. Over the whole of the HAT's life, some ten years, it will have received up to £227m of government grant as well as attracting private finance.

The HAT's pivotal task is the redevelopment of 2,422 high and medium-rise dwellings built in the late 1960s to early 1970s, replacing them with over 1,500 quality homes with gardens. In addition to the construction of new homes, the HAT puts particular importance on the empowerment of HAT residents, involving them in design, planning and decision-making at many levels. Residents sit on the HAT Board, as well as the Boards of O-Regen and the CBHA.

The HAT has consistently met its target of 20% local labour employed in the construction programme, peaking at 30% at the height of the redevelopment programme. New community facilities like 'The Click', an IT learning centre, give residents access to a cyber cafe, Youth Services, employment advice and guidance and information and communications technology training courses. On 31 March 2000 the HAT had helped 3709 residents into jobs or training.

(Photograph: Christa Stadtler, courtesy of Waltham Forest HAT)

6.16 We are helping people realise their aspirations for home ownership through programmes such as the Homebuy Scheme. A new **Starter Home initiative** will help key workers in areas of high demand into home ownership. We also plan to make it easier for people to repair their own homes, while reforms to the homebuying and selling process will make it easier for people to move house.

6.17 We are also seeking to improve the quality of housing services and give social housing tenants meaningful choice about where they live.

Transport

6.18 Efficient and reliable transport is essential to provide people with access to jobs, services and leisure opportunities and enable communities to function effectively. This is dealt with in Chapter 5 as it is a key factor for business location.

Culture, leisure and sport

6.19 A healthy and vibrant cultural, leisure and sporting life enhances cities in a positive way. It helps to create places where people want to be, are proud of and can achieve their potential. It contributes to a city's uniqueness and diversity.

6.20 We want to see a stronger cultural and sporting infrastructure, providing opportunities for everyone, and acting as an educational resource, especially for young people. We are making significant investment in culture and sport, aiming to nurture talent, support excellence, widen access and improve quality of life. New Government schemes such as **Spaces for Sport and Arts** and the development of **Creative Partnerships** will help us to achieve this.

Community legal service

6.21 We aim to provide people, especially the more disadvantaged, with the right level of information and help with legal problems. This radical programme of advice will focus on matters which most affect people's daily lives, such as housing, welfare benefits, employment, discrimination, immigration and money problems. We are encouraging new ideas through local partnerships.

Action to improve services

6.22 The steps we are taking to improve the main services are set out in more detail in pages 114 to 128

at the end of this chapter. For each one we identify:

- the most significant steps **we have taken to improve services so far**;

- how the extra money from **Spending Review 2000** will make a difference for towns and cities;

- the key actions **targeting areas where help is needed most**; and

- the key **Public Service Agreement targets** to be achieved.

A cross-cutting approach to improving services

6.23 The programmes and initiatives summarised in pages 114 to 128 are the building blocks out of which strategies to meet the needs of each local area need to be constructed. But the needs of a particular community in one service area should not be looked at in isolation: they are inter-related with other services and the urban environment and economic issues dealt with in earlier chapters. For example good design can help reduce crime, cultural and sporting facilities can help attract businesses, good education is needed to provide a skilled labour force, and good quality housing contributes to better health.

6.24 To produce the best possible result for the people who live in a particular area we need to look at the whole picture together. That is why Local Strategic Partnerships are central to this White Paper (see Chapter 3, page 34). By working together and with the private, voluntary and community sectors through Local Strategic Partnerships, the agencies responsible for these various services can achieve far more than they could by working alone. And working with the Government Offices and RDAs, they can ensure that national programmes are delivered in ways that meet the differing needs of each area.

6.25 The key to ensuring long term sustainable change is to involve the local community – the people who live and work in an area. Some communities may lack the skills to participate in the process on an equal basis with the statutory agencies and better resourced partners. Initiatives such as the Community Champions Fund can provide a vital first stage for individuals and community groups. Community support organisations, such as Councils for Voluntary Service, Volunteer Bureaux, Community Development Agencies, Development Trusts, are able to provide technical assistance, know how and practical help and take a developmental role.

Location of the 10% most deprived wards in England

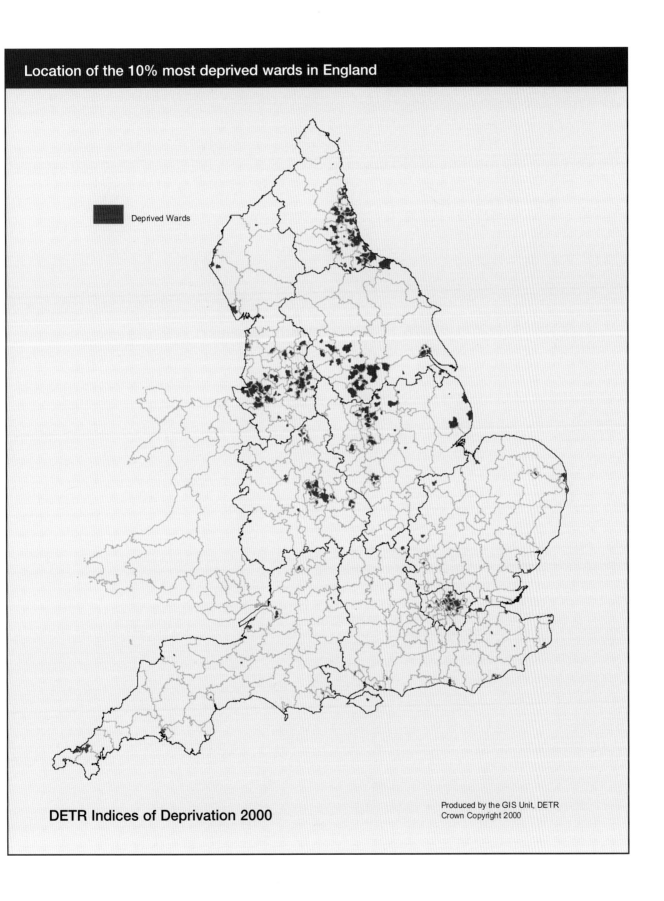

Deprived Wards

DETR Indices of Deprivation 2000

Produced by the GIS Unit, DETR
Crown Copyright 2000

6

6.26   We are also seeking to increase community activity and volunteering through our new **Active Community programme**, which includes £300m to provide small grants for community activities, volunteering programmes and better marketing and promotion of volunteering.

Transforming the most deprived areas

Indices of Deprivation 2000

6.27   Some areas suffer from particularly acute multiple deprivation. The Indices of Deprivation 2000 published by the DETR in August show that many wards suffer from very significant problems. On average, in the 10% most deprived wards:

- 44% of people rely on means tested benefits;

- over 60% of children live in households that are reliant on means tested benefits; and

- nearly a quarter of the relevant adult age group are employment deprived.

6.28   Nearly 7.5 million people or one in seven of the population live in these wards. The proportion of children living in these wards is even higher: it is more than one in six. In 30% of wards in England more than one in three children live in households that depend on means tested benefits.

6.29   The map illustrates the location of these 10% most deprived wards. They are mainly located in cities and in former coal mining areas and seaside towns. There is a clear cluster of very deprived wards in the North East, North West and in London but all regions of England have some very deprived wards.

6.30   In some towns and cities deprivation is spread across the entire area and there are no affluent pockets because most of the better off people associated with these cities live outside the administrative boundaries. In other places severely deprived and prosperous areas co-exist side by side. And, by no means all urban areas suffer from high levels of deprivation.

6.31   The new indices also reveal that even within areas suffering from severe multiple deprivation the relative severity of problems varies. Also, even in the most deprived areas there will be people who are relatively well-off. This evidence gives further weight to the argument that there is not one policy solution to deprived neighbourhoods. Policy responses need to reflect the diversity of the situation.

National Strategy for Neighbourhood Renewal

6.32   The Social Exclusion Unit (SEU) is taking forward work to develop a National Strategy for Neighbourhood Renewal aimed at narrowing the gap between the most deprived neighbourhoods and the rest of the country. These neighbourhoods suffer from a range of interlocking problems – unemployment, high crime, ill health, low educational attainment and poor housing. The success of the National Strategy for Neighbourhood Renewal will be critical to the success of an urban renaissance, and vice versa. But there are important differences. Some deprived neighbourhoods are not in towns or cities, but in rural areas. And it would be wrong to assume that deprivation is a problem in all urban neighbourhoods. Following the SEU 1998 report on deprived neighbourhoods, 18 Policy Action Teams (PATs) were set up to consider various problems and opportunities in deprived neighbourhoods – ranging from jobs and housing management to access to IT. The PATs brought the expertise of frontline workers, residents and academics to bear on policymaking in a new way.

6.33   Drawing on the PAT reports, the Government published a framework draft of the National Strategy in April 2000. This proposed action on four fronts:

- reviving local economies;

- reviving communities;

- ensuring decent services; and

- providing leadership and joint working.

6.34   Underpinning this were a number of key proposed changes to Government policy, including:

- engaging communities more in turning round their neighbourhoods, giving them new leverage over those making decisions that affect them, and making it easier for them to get public funding when they need it;

- focusing core public services – like schools and police – much more on tackling deprivation. Area-based initiatives can only ever help a few areas. But every area is served by public services. If they can deliver more effectively in deprived areas, outcomes can improve everywhere; and

- working collaboratively. Mechanisms, such as Local Strategic Partnerships, were proposed to make joint-working the norm, in a way that draws in the community and other key stakeholders.

6.35 The SEU undertook a major consultation exercise on these ideas, and received an enthusiastic response. The proposals were also examined, as part of Spending Review 2000, in a cross departmental group which was set up to review Government Intervention in Deprived Areas. This helped to influence the way public spending will be directed and used over the next three years. In particular:

- for the first time, departments are setting specific targets to start narrowing the gap between the most deprived areas and the rest of the country. These cover each of the four key outcomes of the National Strategy for Neighbourhood Renewal – education, employment, health and crime together with housing;

- to ensure that these targets are delivered, each department will review its funding allocation processes to ensure that a generous proportion of the additional resources announced in Spending Review 2000 reaches deprived areas. As a first step, local authorities covering the most deprived areas will benefit from a new **Neighbourhood Renewal Fund (NRF)**, worth £100m in 2001/02, £300m in 2002/03, and £400m in 2003/04, to allow them to make a start on improving services in poorer communities;

- building on the new Community Planning duty and the wide range of existing cross-sectoral partnerships, service providers across the country will be encouraged to establish Local Strategic Partnerships, bringing together the public, private, voluntary and community sectors, matching investment with reform. This will also form part of a wider drive to encourage the rationalisation of existing partnerships into simpler and less bureaucratic structures. LSPs in the most deprived areas will receive start-up funding from the New Deal for Communities to help them engage effectively with the community and voluntary sector interests; and

- government initiatives targeted at specific areas, such as New Deal for Communities (see paragraph 6.39), are being reviewed to ensure that their role is complementary to refocused main services.

6.36 We have just launched consultation documents on both the Neighbourhood Renewal Fund and on Local Strategic Partnership Guidance. These are closely linked as we are proposing that the commitment to establish an LSP will be a pre-condition for the 88 authorities receiving NRF.

Key PSA targets – tackling deprivation

Education
Reduce to zero the number of LEAs where fewer than a set percentage of pupils achieve level 4 in each of the Key Stage 2 english and maths tests.

Increase the percentage of pupils obtaining five or more GCSEs at grades A*-C (or equivalent) with at least 38% to achieve this standard in every LEA by 2004.

Employment
Over the three years to 2004, an increase in the employment rates of disadvantaged areas and groups (people with disabilities, lone parents, ethnic minorities and the over 50s, the 30 local authority districts with the poorest initial labour market position) – taking account of the economic cycle – and a reduction in the difference between their employment rates and the overall rate.

Crime
Reduce domestic burglary by 25% (with no local authority area having more than three times the national average) by 2005.

Health
Narrow the health gap in childhood and throughout life between socio-economic groups and between the most deprived areas and the rest of the country. Specific national targets will be developed in consultation with external stakeholders and experts early in 2001.

Housing
Ensure that all social housing is of a decent standard by 2010 by reducing the number of households living in social housing that does not meet these standards by a third between 2001 and 2004; with most of the improvements taking place in the most deprived local authority areas as part of a comprehensive regeneration strategy.

6.37 An **action plan for neighbourhood renewal** will be published shortly, setting out in detail how the Government will work with local partners to help make neighbourhood renewal happen.

6.38   This chapter has concentrated on the provision of key public services but services provided by the private sector, such as shops, banks and leisure facilities, are equally important to all communities. For this reason the draft National Strategy looked also at ways in which the provision of financial services and shops in deprived areas could be improved. There will be a £5m per annum fund to sustain and improve post offices and associated retail facilities in deprived urban areas.

Neighbourhood programmes

New Deal for Communities

6.39   Valuable lessons have been learned from the New Deal for Communities programme. This focuses on jobs, improving health, tackling crime and raising educational achievement. Currently there are 17 pathfinder areas with partnerships between local people, community and voluntary groups, public agencies, local authorities and business. 22 further partnerships have been established under Round 2.

New Deal for Communities project: East Manchester Cross Tenure Neighbourhood Nuisance Team

This project provides a cross tenure neighbourhood nuisance team to work with social and private landlords and all residents in East Manchester to tackle anti-social behaviour and neighbour nuisance consistently in all housing tenures. Strategies will be used to challenge anti-social behaviour, by diverting individuals away from nuisance using a multi-agency approach, or by taking serious offenders to court. The project will improve residents' confidence in the area and reduce fear of crime.

New funding for New Deal for Communities

6.40   An extra £200m was allocated in the Spending Review to the new ventures under the New Deal for Communities programme, on top of around £2 billion committed to the 39 partnerships.

6.41   This will:

- support pilot schemes to test neighbourhood management experiments, which will involve neighbourhood managers working with service providers and others to ensure that the needs of local residents and communities are met;

- promote community involvement at the local and neighbourhood level; and

- set up a National Centre for Neighbourhood Renewal which will promote best practice and improve the skills and expertise of those involved.

Neighbourhood wardens

6.42   Neighbourhood wardens are an important part of the neighbourhood renewal agenda. We have set up a new unit within DETR to promote the concept of wardens, to offer advice and to allocate government grant to warden schemes. £13.5m is available for the first round. 50 schemes have achieved funding support and a further 40 schemes are likely to be funded early in 2001. The aim is to use wardens to improve the quality of life by promoting community safety, helping with environmental improvements and housing management and contributing to community development.

Neighbourhood Wardens from Wansbeck, Northumberland reporting environmental damage.

Sure Start

6.43 We are spending £1.4 billion over five years to 2003/04 on Sure Start local programmes in 500 deprived areas. They will reach one third of all poor children under four. They will:

- promote the physical, emotional, intellectual and social development of children to ensure that they are ready to flourish when they get to school;

- involve the local community, including parents, voluntary and statutory providers; and

- pioneer new and innovative ways of working which will be adopted more widely by service providers.

6

ACTION TO DELIVER QUALITY SERVICES
1: Education

1.   Good education is vital to everyone. It has a particular role in revitalising our cities by:

- reversing the trend for families to move out; and

- building effective urban communities.

Government action to transform education

2.   Improving education has been our top priority since 1997. Already we have taken great strides, in particular by:

- raising standards in primary schools through **National Literacy and Numeracy Strategies** with 11-year-olds improving their 2000 test results by 18% in both maths and english compared with four years earlier. Improvement has been fastest in inner city areas – the lowest performing area now exceeds what was the national average in 1996;

- launching a programme – **Excellence in Cities** – specifically directed at transforming secondary education in our major cities. Its main strands are now also being piloted at primary level. It is currently spending some £120m a year – excluding capital – so that city children are educated just as well as children anywhere else in the country;

- reducing class sizes in all our primary schools; and

- monitoring more effectively through OFSTED inspections, the attainment and achievements of school pupils by ethnicity and the implementation of race equality strategies.

3.   We have also taken other steps for each age-group:

- guaranteed a free early education place for all four year olds and introduced a major expansion for three year olds, with 120,000 extra **free places** for both three and four year olds;

- introduced a Foundation Stage and Early Learning Goals to enable three to six year olds to develop key skills and enjoy the best possible start to their education;

- set up, with local authorities, partnerships to plan and monitor childcare and education for the youngest children;

- encouraged the growth of nursery education and childcare facilities on the same site;

- linked education with health and other services as mentioned above, by setting up '***Sure Start***': partnerships (see paragraph 6.43);

- brought together schools, local authorities, businesses, parents and community groups to find imaginative new ways to raise standards in **education action zones**; and

- expanded alternative, community-based learning through the Adult and Community Learning Fund, the Neighbourhood Support Fund and the Community Champions Fund.

Excellence in Cities programme

Working in partnership, Excellence in Cities Local Education Authorities and their schools are putting in place:

- enhanced educational opportunities for gifted and talented children;

- access to learning mentors to help children overcome barriers to learning;

- Learning Support Units for disruptive children at risk of exclusion;

- City Learning Centres to bring state of the art technology to teaching and learning;

- a network of urban Beacon and Specialist schools;

- small Education Action Zones to provide focused action covering individual secondary schools and their primary feeder schools; and

- early signs are of success in improving raising expectations and improved pupil behaviour.

---

continued

Developing enhanced opportunities

120 gifted and talented pupils experienced a day with leading academics who came to London to deliver lectures, including Sir Walter Bodmer on genetics and biotechnology, Dr Emma Smith on why we study Shakespeare and a lecture on the logic of maps. After this taste of university life, most of the pupils signed up for a return visit to the academics at Oxford University.

Further investment in education

4.   In the recent spending review, we committed an extra £10 billion for education and training over the three years to 2003/04, building on existing initiatives. Within the national standard setting agenda we are:

* extending our national **literacy and numeracy** strategy to cover **secondary** schools and continuing it for another three years at primary level;

* expanding **catch-up programmes** to help children who fall behind their class-mates;

* boosting pupils' access to **computers**;

* launching the first City Academies – publicly funded independent schools supported by business and the Voluntary sector;

* supporting all 13-19 year olds through the **Connexions Service** by providing information, advice and guidance about learning, vocational and personal development opportunities to help make the transition to adulthood and working life. It will be a 'universal' service with additional help targeted on those whose needs are greatest. A network of personal advisers will broker and co-ordinate the delivery of specialist support services, where appropriate. The service – which is currently being piloted in a number of areas – will start to be rolled out across England from April 2001; and

* developing academic and work-linked routes to learning which meet all young people's needs, and working to embed good practice in teaching disadvantaged young people.

Education measures in deprived areas

5.   These measures will raise standards everywhere. We also recognise that urban areas of disadvantage need special attention, so we are:

* using a new **£450m Children's fund over three years** to tackle child poverty and social exclusion. £380m will help vulnerable five to 13 year olds before they hit a crisis, to break the cycle of disadvantage. Communities will meet their local needs through mentoring, counselling, and advice on parenting. A £70m local network of children's funds will invest in community and voluntary groups to address local problems. Focusing on children and their families, it will emphasise young people's own hopes and views;

* expanding the **'Excellence in Cities'** programme so that by 2001 it will cover nearly 60 authorities across all our major cities and by 2003/04 will be funded by more than £300m;

continued

- tackling low educational standards wherever they occur, by bringing the benefits of the Excellence in Cities programme to clusters of schools in disadvantaged communities outside the major cities. e.g. coastal towns and former industrial communities;

- targeting the major expansion (through £1.13 billion funding over five years) of **free early education for three year olds** on areas of greatest social need. By March 2002, 66% of three year olds will be able to find a place. However by September 2004, there will be a free place for all three year olds;

- creating new childcare places in nurseries by funding building work in 75 authorities with the areas of greatest social need through the **New Deal for Schools**;

- launching a three year, £150m **Excellence Challenge**, so that more young people from inner city areas will go into higher education;

- spreading neighbourhood learning by enabling the local Learning and Skills Council to implement the recommendations of the Skills Policy Action Team.

- re-engaging disaffected 13-19 year olds living in some of the most deprived areas back into education, training and employment through the **Neighbourhood Support Fund**. The £60m Fund over three years will support about 700 community and voluntary based projects in 40 priority local authority areas in England.

Key education PSA targets

- Increase the percentage of 11 year olds at or above the standard of literacy and numeracy for their age. Reduce to zero by 2004 the number of LEAs where fewer than a set percentage of pupils achieve level 4 in each of the key stage 2 english and maths tests, reinforcing progress already made. This will mainly help pupils in urban areas;

- Increase the percentage of 14 year olds at or above the standard of literacy, numeracy, Information and Communications Technology and science for their age. Subject to consultation, by 2007, 85% to achieve level 5 or above in each of the Key Stage 3 tests in English, maths and ICT, and 80% in Science;

- By 2004, increase the percentage of pupils obtaining five or more GCSEs at grades A* to C (or equivalent) to at least 38% in every authority;

- Cut by 750,000 the number of adults who have literacy or numeracy problems by 2004;

- Make significant year on year progress towards fair access to higher education, increasing the opportunity for access towards 50% of young people by the end of the decade.

1.   Good health and well being are fundamental to all our lives. In addition to policies on the wider determinants of health we are modernising the National Health Service (NHS) and social services to benefit everyone, with specific measures to help the most vulnerable, who often live in our urban areas.

2.   We have put in place:

- the **Health Act 1999** which enabled local councils and the NHS to work more closely;

- **Health Improvement Programmes** which will ensure that LAs, NHS bodies and the public are included in, and are able to make a real difference in, tackling health inequalities;

- **personal medical services pilots**, giving vulnerable people better access to primary health care by allowing locally negotiated contracts which are more focused on local patients' health needs;

- **local development schemes**, to help GPs target vulnerable sections of the population and tackle health problems arising from social difficulties, through model schemes;

- **NHS Direct**, a telephone service staffed by health professionals, which provides people at home with round the clock information and advice on health; and

- **Quality Protects**, a programme to improve the life chances of the most vulnerable children in our society: those children looked after by local authorities, in the child protection system and other children in need.

The NHS Plan

3.   The NHS Plan, published in July, reaffirmed the Government's faith in the NHS and its determination to secure fast, modern and convenient health services for everyone in the country. Backed by unprecedented levels of investment, the NHS is embarking on a period of change which will transform the way that health care is delivered in England's towns and cities and will signal a new drive to tackle the health problems of people living in deprived urban communities.

4.   The NHS Plan builds on the foundations of three years of change that are altering the relationship between the local NHS and the communities that it serves.

- The establishment of **Primary Care Groups** has put local doctors and their teams in the lead in developing services that are better suited to the people they serve.

- Health Authorities are now required to draw up **Health Improvement Programmes** setting out how the local NHS, working with all local partners, can improve both health and health services in their locality.

These new mechanisms, devolving power and planning to the locality, will allow urban NHS services to be much more finely tuned to the needs of the urban populations they serve.

5.   Towns and cities have benefited from further extensions of NHS services in recent years. NHS Direct offers easier access to NHS professionals over the phone, 24 hours a day, 365 days a year. NHS Direct Online (www.nhsdirect.nhs.uk) harnesses the internet to give another gateway to NHS services.

6.   These measures will enhance NHS services in urban settings, and they have been augmented by specific measures to support the modernisation of NHS services in areas which need particular support.

- The Government has established 26 **Health Action Zones**, the majority of them focused on areas of urban deprivation, to tackle health inequalities and modernise services by addressing key priorities such as heart disease, cancer and mental health, as well as tackling the social and economic causes of ill health.

- £300m of lottery money is being targeted on economically disadvantaged areas to develop a network of **Healthy Living Centres**, providing deprived communities with free and affordable facilities such as gyms, childcare, adult education, and a range of health services.

continued

7. There have been important innovations to improve the range of services that family doctors and their teams can provide to patients in towns and cities.

- **Personal Medical Service Pilots** have given vulnerable people better access to primary health care by allowing locally negotiated contracts which are better focused on local patient's health needs.

- In hospital care, nine **Cancer Collaboratives** have been established, pioneering ways of reducing delays in the diagnosis, treatment and care of cancer, providing "one stop shops" for patients, with tests and results available on the same day.

8. England's towns and cities have also seen the start of an unprecedented programme of renewal in the physical fabric of the NHS. Every run down accident and emergency department in the country is being modernised. After decades of decay, new hospitals are now being built in England's towns and cities. Since May 1997, 34 major hospital building projects worth over £3.6 billion have been approved to proceed.

Neptune Health Park. A healthy living centre in Tipton, West Midlands, built on reclaimed brownfield land, which has been a catalyst for the revitalisation of the town centre.
(Photograph courtesy of Sandwell Metropolitan Borough Council)

Reducing inequalities

9. Throughout this programme of investment and reform, the NHS has been striving to tackle the inequalities that exist between and within different parts of the country.

- Health Action Zones and Healthy Living Centres are important parts of that effort.

- The Government has also invested money in **Local Development Schemes** to help GPs target vulnerable sections of the population and tackle health problems arising from social difficulties.

- A network of **NHS walk-in-centres**, including Birmingham, London, Manchester, Newcastle, Norwich, Peterborough, Sheffield and York is extending the ways in which people in cities can access high quality care.

- Initiatives are under way in a number of cities to improve people's access to affordable and healthy food, seeking to open up the "food deserts" that can exist in socially blighted urban communities.

10. More generally, there are important initiatives under way to end the postcode lottery for treatment and drugs in the NHS.

- The National Institute for Clinical Evidence, The Cancer Plan and the National Service Frameworks for Heart Disease and for Mental Health are building up a clear body of guidance about the level and quality of care that all NHS patients can expect, regardless of where they live.

- Substantial new resources underpin that guidance and new systems for ensuring that standards are met, such as the Commission for Health Improvement, are monitoring and enforcing those standards.

11. As part of **The NHS Plan**:

- by 2004 all patients will have guaranteed access to a primary care professional within 24 hours and to a GP appointment within 48 hours;

- by the end of 2005 the maximum waiting time for any outpatient appointment will be three months and for inpatients six months;

- all outpatient and inpatient elective admissions will be pre-booked by 2005;

- long waits in accident and emergency departments will be ended;

continued

118

- a big expansion of breast screening programmes with screening for all women aged 65-70;

- rapid access to chest pain clinics across the country by 2003;

- by 2004 there will be a £900m package of intermediate care services to allow older people to live more independent lives;

- nursing care in nursing homes will be provided free by the NHS. Statutory guidance will be issued to councils to tackle the current unacceptable variations in charges for home care;

- there will be 335 mental health teams to provide an immediate response to crisis;

- participation of problem drug users in drug treatment programmes will be increased by 55% by 2004 and 100% by 2008, impacting both on health and crime; and

- four to six year old children will have fruit freely available in schools to improve their diet.

Health Action Zone

Bradford HAZ launched in 1998 covers an area of 486,000 people. The main focus of its work is improving the health of people facing the greatest health inequalities, mainly in inner city areas and within the minority ethnic communities. Community involvement is also a key feature. Achievements include:

- 4,000 patients receiving treatment at neighbourhood diabetic clinics;

- Primary Care Groups providing more outreach clinics and intermediate care, with eight extra GPs working in the most disadvantaged areas to support single-handed GPs; and

- drug prevention and other health initiatives targeting 12,000 primary school children.

Key health and social services PSA targets

- Narrow the health gap in childhood and throughout life between socio-economic groups and between the most deprived areas and the rest of the country. Specific national targets will be developed in consultation with external stakeholders and experts in 2001.

- Transform the health and social care system so that it produces faster, fairer services that deliver better health and tackle health inequalities.

- Reduce substantially the mortality rates from major killers by 2010; from heart diseases by at least 40% in people under 75; from cancer by at least 20% in people under 75; and from suicide and undetermined injury by at least 20%.

- Reduce the maximum wait for an outpatient appointment to three months and the maximum wait for inpatient treatment to six months by the end of 2005.

- Provide high quality pre-admission and rehabilitation care to older people to help them live as independently as possible.

- Improve the life chances of children in care by improving the level of education, training and employment outcomes for care leavers aged 19 by March 2004; by improving the educational attainment of children and young people in care; by giving them the care and guidance needed to narrow the gap by 2004 between the proportion of children in care who are cautioned and their peers; and to maximising the contribution adoption can make to providing permanent families for children.

6

ACTION TO DELIVER QUALITY SERVICES
3: Crime

1.   The problems of crime and disorder hit urban areas the hardest. Although crime across England and Wales has come down by 10% since 1997, the risk of being the victim of a burglary is about 50% greater and the risk of being a victim of car crime a third higher in inner cities than the national average. Crime restricts people's everyday freedoms and, as people and businesses move out, so communities become even poorer. Tackling crime must therefore be an essential feature of plans to regenerate our urban areas.

New powers to help local communities

2.   To help local communities fight back against crime we need to ensure all those involved in the community – from schools to hospitals, local businesses to tenants groups – are involved in efforts to cut crime.

- 376 **crime and disorder reduction partnerships** are now up and running in England and Wales, bringing together police, local authorities, probation services and others to pool local efforts in the fight against crime.

- **Radical reforms of the youth justice system** have been introduced nationwide, with new Youth Offending Teams in every area of the country.

- **Anti-Social Behaviour Orders** are helping the police and local authorities tackle the persistent misbehaviour of particular individuals in communities – well over 100 ASBOs have been made by the courts, many in urban areas.

- **New measures to tackle disorder and alcohol-related violence** have been proposed, including fixed penalty notices for loutish behaviour, extra powers to help the police deal with rogue pubs and controls on on-street drinking. A new framework for **licensing** is needed which allows sensible drinking whilst also ensuring that trouble spot areas are tackled by a combination of police enforcement and licensing decisions.

- We also recognise that good design of buildings and the way buildings and public spaces are laid out can help prevent crime. We are:

  – making crime prevention a key objective for planning; and

  – reviewing and updating advice on "Planning Out Crime".

Focus on local crime reduction

3.   An ambitious £400m crime reduction programme is boosting innovative work in local communities, many in high-crime urban areas. The programme includes:

- a national scheme to fund projects in areas containing **two million homes** in crime hot-spots to **reduce domestic burglary**. Areas containing 816,000 households have already received help;

- the **biggest ever expansion of CCTV** schemes the country has seen – over 350 schemes have been offered funding so far;

- programmes to prevent children from becoming involved in crime, and **to reduce school truancy and exclusions using powers in the Crime and Disorder Act**;

- funding to support the establishment of **neighbourhood warden schemes** to complement the work of the police and local authorities (see paragraph 6.42); and

- providing **drug-arrest referral schemes** in all police custody suites to encourage drug-misusing offenders into treatment and out of crime. By the end of 2000 every police custody suite should have a drugs worker on site to assess offenders and refer them straight to treatment if appropriate.

continued

Investing in the police

4. The police have our full support in helping to make urban communities safer. There will be a 21% increase in spending on the police from 2001/02 to 2003/04. Amongst other things this will help increase recruitment and help the service benefit from the latest developments in anti-crime technology. As a result, we are:

- boosting police recruitment with a Crime Fighting Fund to allow forces to take on an **extra 9,000 officers** over and above the numbers planned for this financial year and the following two; and

Two constables provide a friendly and reassuring presence on patrol in the streets of Reading (Photograph: Richard White, courtesy of Thames Valley Police).

- investing in **police technology** to help the police reduce crime and bring more offenders to justice, including £500m on a new secure radio communications system, £185m to expand the DNA database, and extra support to improve IT systems.

Tackling drugs

5. Much of crime is drug-related. Research from five inner urban areas showed that up to a third of those arrested by the police were recent users of hard drugs. The Government has embarked on a 10 year strategy aimed at:

- reducing the proportion of people under 25 who use Class A drugs by 25% by 2005 and by 50% by 2008;

- increasing participation of problem drug users in treatment programmes by 55% by 2004 and by 100% by 2008;

- reducing levels of repeat offending amongst drug misusing offenders by 25% by 2005 and by 50% by 2008;

- new Drug Treatment and Testing Orders are now available to the courts across the country to help drug-misusing offenders get off drugs and out of crime;

- repeat class-A dealers now face minimum seven-year prison sentences;

- over the next three years the Government will be investing an additional £558m to buy extra treatment places, more drugs education in schools and a crack down on drug traffickers; by 2004 that should be sufficient to buy thousands more treatment places in the community and inside prison. Every prison will have a specialist drugs dog. The police will be given resources to test the people they arrest so that they can identify at an early stage and better monitor those who misuse drugs; and

- the Government will be setting up a new Confiscation Agency staffed by highly trained financial investigators and others to maximise the revenue seized from drug traffickers and other career criminals.

6

Key crime PSA targets

- Reduce the key recorded crime categories of:

  – vehicle crime by 30% by 2004.
  – domestic burglary by 25% with no local authority area having a rate more than three times the national average, by 2005.
  – robbery in our principal cities by 14% by 2005.

- Increase the number and proportion of recorded crimes for which an offender is brought to justice.

- Reduce the rate of reconviction:
  – of offenders punished by imprisonment or community supervision by 5% by 2004, compared to the predicted rate.
  – of all young offenders by 5% by 2004, compared to the predicted rate.

1. Our towns and cities must be places where people want to live. Having a decent home is a fundamental requirement. Good quality housing means more than just attractive homes. Decent homes contribute to Government objectives in a number of ways. They:

- give people a stronger sense of security and identity;

- strengthen communities;

- protect health; and

- provide a better setting in which people can raise families and promote educational achievement.

Properly designed developments can also discourage crime.

2. Chapter 4 discusses how the planning system can ensure that houses are built in the right places, and that their design fits in with the surroundings. But what matters most to individuals is that homes are pleasant places to live in, and that they can move easily when necessary.

3. But too many people in our towns and cities do not have a decent home. In 1996 five million homes in urban areas – 32% – failed to meet the set standard of decency. Our housing policy is designed to realise our objective that everyone should have the opportunity of a decent home. People will not want to live in towns and cities if they do not have access to a decent home. Across all types of housing, owned or rented, private or public, our policies are intended to deliver improvements in quality and a fairer market that allow people to make real choices about their homes, that support people moving into work and self-dependence, and that protect the vulnerable.

Better Urban Housing

(Photograph: Dennis Gilbert, courtesy of Pollard, Thomas and Edwards)

Architects Pollard Thomas & Edwards put together a development team, led by Galliard Homes working with the Guiness Trust and Islington and Shoreditch Housing Association, for this typical inner city regeneration site. This is a high density development, providing 31 homes for private sale, eight for shared ownership and 28 at affordable rents.

23 of the 67 homes are houses with gardens: the remaining 44 are flats, including ten flats with private patios. All above ground flats have balconies. The layout is a perimeter development, enclosing secure private and communal open space, including a toddlers' playground.

This is a convincing demonstration that skilled designers, working closely with supportive clients and local planning officers, can produce housing of an appropriate urban scale and type for an integrated mix of tenures and household sizes. High standards of design, construction and planning mean that this development should be a social as well as a commercial success.

6

4. Housing expectations have changed radically over the last twenty years. Owner occupiers represent nearly 70% of households now, compared with around 30% in 1950. And around 90% say they aspire to own their own home. Single person households have increased 20% over the last ten years to over 6 million and are forecast to rise to 8.5 million by 2021. The labour market makes increasing demands on mobility that may require us to move more often.

5. Our worst housing problems can be found in urban areas. Mistakes in the past, and a history of underinvestment in social housing, have led to a backlog of repair work in the social sector and the concentration of some of the poorest and most vulnerable people in our society. In some areas older and more unpopular housing has been abandoned as people move out to city fringes. In other areas, demand for housing is high and people wanting to buy their own home can find it difficult to get a foot on the ladder.

Housing Green Paper

6. Our housing policy forms a comprehensive strategy to address this range of issues. It was put forward in the Housing Green Paper "Quality and Choice: A decent home for all" and following the spending review we announced an extra £1.8 billion for housing over the next three years to deliver this strategy. This is on top of the extra £5 billion announced for housing as a result of our Capital Receipts Initiative and the Comprehensive Spending Review.

- We are raising the **quality of social housing**. We are committed to tackling the £19 billion backlog of repairs and modernisation work. We have set ourselves a target to make all social housing decent in ten years, and in July we announced resources for the next three years that set us on course towards this target. We will achieve this by giving local authorities more money to spend, by encouraging the transfer of more stock to Registered Social Landlords (RSLs) and by the use of private finance.

- We are also raising the **quality of housing services**. We are introducing a new financial framework for housing to improve the way housing stock is managed. And we have put in place a Best Value in Housing framework, backed up by a new Housing Inspectorate, to encourage local authorities and RSLs to improve the services they offer to tenants. The introduction of tenant participation compacts will ensure that tenants have the opportunity to influence the housing decisions that effect them and their community.

- Good quality **housing management** is an important tool for local authorities in improving the quality of life on our more deprived estates. We are encouraging authorities to adopt a more corporate approach to their housing services by ensuring housing is fully integrated into the authorities wider strategy and other services, such as regeneration, planning and health.

Renewal areas

Renewal areas, which are used to tackle concentrations of poor quality housing, are often a key part of local regeneration strategies. Used with other regeneration measures, they can help prevent decline by making residential areas safer and more attractive to live in. There are currently 132 renewal areas in England, in which over £1.75 billion will be invested over their lifetimes. In Rochdale, the Castleton and Whitworth Road renewal areas, which are now complete, have helped improve 930 homes and to maintain a stable market for the mainly terraced housing in the area. During their ten-year lives, the two schemes have stimulated a number of voluntary initiatives which still enjoy widespread community support.

- We plan to make it easier to help **people repair their own homes**. Our Quality Mark scheme will give home owners greater confidence in employing builders. We will introduce reforms to give local authorities freedom to help more homeowners who cannot afford to do their own repairs. And we will make it easier for local authorities to carry out area renewal to tackle the problems relating to low demand.

continued

- We are helping people realise their aspirations of **home ownership**. Home ownership promotes a culture of opportunity, choice and self-reliance and gives people a stake in their neighbourhoods. A stable and sound economy is giving people the confidence to buy their own homes. But we are providing other support too. Programmes such as the Homebuy scheme are helping people into partial home ownership that can pave the way for full ownership later.

- In addition we have announced a **starter home initiative** to help key workers, such as policemen, nurses, teachers, in areas of high demand into home ownership so that they are not priced out of communities to whom their services are vital. This initiative will play a key role in promoting sustainable communities and improving towns and cities.

The Starter Home Initiative

In July we announced an extra £250m to fund this initiative over the next three years. This is additional to existing spending plans and separate from the Housing Corporation's Approved Development Programme for other affordable housing.

Full details will be announced soon and we will invite registered social landlords and others to submit proposals for schemes. Our aim is to have new schemes up and running during 2001.

We are keen to encourage employers of key workers to play a part in schemes, perhaps in partnership with local authorities, registered social landlords, developers, lenders and others.

We intend to set broad criteria, including a general definition of key workers as those whose services are essential to the local community and who must live within or close to that community.

- **Empowering residents** to make decisions about the homes and communities they live in is central to building sustainable communities. We want to give local authority tenants greater choice in where they live and are making available £11m to local authorities to pilot new style lettings schemes.

- We want to give tenants in the private rented sector greater assurance that the **landlords** they choose will meet higher standards. Our proposals will help existing landlords raise their standards, encourage more investment in the sector, and crack down on the minority of disreputable landlords.

- Our **reforms to the homebuying and selling process** will make it easier for people to move house. Those who are more confident that they can sell without hassle will be more ready to move to find and benefit the economy as a whole.

- We will provide more affordable homes to rent by nearly doubling funding channelled through the Housing Corporations, with an extra £872m over the next three years.

- We are providing £137m for a new **safer communities housing fund** and increasing resources for grants for disabled facilities and to home improvement agencies, to improve housing quality and support for the most vulnerable people in society.

- We are making available £153m for our new **Supporting People** programme which will bring together support services for vulnerable people.

- We have established a new strategy for tackling **rough sleeping**, with a target to reduce the number of people sleeping rough to a third of its current level by 2002.

7.   All these proposals contribute to a housing market for all. There is no place any more for old-fashioned segregation of housing. We need to move towards sustainable communities where no stigma is attached to certain forms of tenure, and all can enjoy decent surroundings.

Key housing PSA target

- Ensure that all social housing is of a decent standard by 2010 with the number of families living in non-decent social housing falling by one third by 2004, and with most of the improvement taking place in the most deprived local authority areas as part of a comprehensive regeneration strategy.

ACTION TO DELIVER QUALITY SERVICES
5: Culture, leisure and sport

1. Cultural, leisure and sporting activities are an essential ingredient to a lively and vibrant town or city stimulating social and economic well-being. Building on existing strengths of cultural communities they attract people to live in or visit an area and encourage businesses to locate there. Whether it is a local football team, the libraries, museums or galleries, or people's access to leisure centres, cinemas, local cafes and bars, these things help to define the character of a place. They:

- are a source of civic pride and a positive way of celebrating racial and other forms of diversity;

- can be an important factor in economic success;

- promote and develop lifelong learning; and

- can help tackle community safety and promote social inclusion by enabling more people to participate in sports and cultural activities in the most deprived neighbourhoods.

2. Culture in its many forms touches all facets of urban life. The Government, working with many partners, seeks to ensure a healthy cultural infrastructure, to which there is access for the many and not the few, and to make the most of its use as an educational resource.

Government action to improve cultural/leisure/sporting activities

3. Many of our urban areas already have successful cultural, leisure and sporting facilities with a thriving programme of events and activities. The impact of these on regeneration will be demonstrated by the Beacon Councils for Regenerating through Culture, Sport and Tourism, expected to be announced in January 2001. In other places there is more that could be done. To help with this the Government has already:

- scrapped entry charges to **national museums and galleries** in England for children and pensioners;

Sporting Excellence

(Photograph courtesy of Sandwell Metropolitan Borough Council)

This 7.5 hectare former landfill site had to have 14 mineshafts capped prior to its regeneration from an obsolete leisure centre to an academy of sporting excellence in the Black Country.

Funding of remedial works by Tipton City Challenge stimulated a £5.3m development, including 12 indoor and outdoor tennis courts, a floodlit eight lane athletics track, new football and cricket pitches and a top class home for 16 local voluntary groups.

The funding cocktail included the Lawn Tennis Association, Lottery Sports Fund, Football Trust and English Partnerships.

Added value was provided in the form of a spectacular 18 metre-high twin arch structure which was engineered using local skills from a company which had its production capacity extended with the assistance of City Challenge.

- through the Arts Council of England's **'New Audiences'** programme, targeted communities with fewer opportunities for artistic experiences, many of them in urban areas, achieving over one million first time attendees;

continued

- encouraged local authorities to take a more strategic approach to the provision of culture and sport in their area by developing **Local Cultural Strategies**; and

- started the competition to select the **UK's Capital of Culture** for 2008.

Libraries

Libraries play an important part in lifelong learning and are a highly valued community resource. The Government is creating a People's Network bringing all the UK public libraries online and linking them to the National Grid for Learning by the end of 2002. £170m of Lottery funding will implement the Network, train staff and digitise material for use. The People's Network is part of the Government's broader UK Online initiative as mentioned in Chapter 5.

Further measures

4.   In addition, this year the Government has announced that it is:

- putting in place the **Spaces for Sports and Arts Scheme** – £130m over the next two years for arts and sports facilities in primary schools, in targeted local education authorities, with access for the public after school hours;

- developing **national standards for public libraries**, covering location, access and opening hours;

- developing an innovative **Culture On-line** service to improve access to culture and the arts through the internet and other electronic media; and

- making it even cheaper for certain groups to get into **national museums and galleries** that charge for admission by extending free admission to major benefit holders and people with disabilities and introducing a £1 admission charge for others.

Improving access to culture/leisure/sport in deprived areas

5.   These activities will improve access to culture, leisure and sport everywhere, but we need to give particular attention to the most deprived areas of cities and towns. This is being done through:

- developing proposals for new **Creative Partnerships** to ensure that every school pupil in targeted deprived areas has access to an innovative programme of cultural and creative opportunities – £40m over two years;

- the Arts Council of England ensuring that arts organisations in regular receipt of public funds demonstrate a firm commitment to extending the impact of their work in relation to the communities they serve, taking a partnership approach;

- the establishment by Sport England of **Sports Action Zones** where basic sports provision falls below acceptable standards; and

- reallocation by Sport England of half of its Lottery Community Projects Fund to areas of greatest need.

Using arts and sport to tackle crime and anti-social behaviour

Sport 2000 based in Derbyshire, works in 20 areas with significant problems of youth crime and disorder to provide training and employment for 50 16-25 year olds and facilities for young people to participate in sports and recreational activities. It also provides education on community safety issues and promotes a drug free lifestyle.

Key culture/leisure/sport PSA targets

- Raise significantly, year on year, the average time spent on sport and physical activity by those aged five to 16.

- Introduce at least 12 Creative Partnerships by March 2004 targeted on deprived areas.

- Increase by 500,000 by 2004 the number of people experiencing the arts.

- Ensure all public libraries have internet access by end 2002.

- Increase numbers of children attending national Museums and Galleries by a third by 2004.

6

ACTION TO DELIVER QUALITY SERVICES
6: Community legal service

1. Too many people living in urban areas suffer because they are unable to access the advice and legal help they need for their particular problem. We therefore set up the Community Legal Service (CLS) in April to improve access to the services people need through help and advice on issues such as housing, debt, welfare benefits, employment and immigration.

2. The CLS includes:

- Community Legal Service Partnerships, which already cover two thirds of the country, are responsible for developing the network of local service providers, including private practice solicitors, Citizens Advice Bureaux, law centres and other advice agencies from the not-for profit sector, and local council services. The providers in each network operate an active referral system, enabling a client to receive the right type of advice quickly.

- the CLS Quality Mark, which gives the public confidence that the services provided by each outlet have met n agreed quality standard.

- the CLS website, 'Just Ask!', provides functions that improve access to relevant advice and information on the Internet, and directs people to local and national advice and information providers.

Key Lord Chancellor's Department performance targets

- Reduce the proportion of disputes which are resolved by resort to the courts.

- Increase the number of people who receive suitable assistance in priority areas of law involving fundamental rights or social exclusion, by 5% by 2004.

Making it happen: action for all

Contents

Places for people

7.1 This White Paper is about making all areas of our towns, cities and suburbs truly 'places for people' – inclusive communities in which all can enjoy a good quality of life and achieve their full potential.

7.2 Government at all levels needs to lead and enable the process of change involving individuals, local communities, businesses and the voluntary sector fully in deciding the way forward and bringing about change.

7.3 There is no single solution to improving towns and cities, whether building on success or rejuvenating less successful areas. One of the strongest lessons from the past is that policies and programmes need to be comprehensive and tailored to circumstance.

The foundation for delivery

7.4 This White Paper completes the first phase of the Government's long term programme for improving and reviving our towns and cities. It is based on a wide ranging debate about the future, particularly drawing on the work of the Urban Task Force and extensive research and analysis in the Cities Programme. It brings together the experience of the last three years in which a wide range of new policies and programmes have been developed and implemented.

7.5 The White Paper establishes a comprehensive framework for action within which we can drive forward existing policies and programmes and the new measures announced here supported by the additional resources for public services from next April.

7.6   In this first three years we have:

- created the basis for a new strategic approach in every area through the Regional Development Agencies and a reformed and modernised local government;

- reformed and modernised the planning regime so that new principles supporting the urban renaissance apply to housing, town centres and the re-use of land; and begun to apply those principles in Regional Planning Guidance;

- set out long term strategies for:

  - improving public transport, reducing congestion and ensuring better maintained roads through the 10 Year Transport Plan;

  - raising the quality of social housing, housing services and management and helping people into home ownership through the Housing Green Paper;

  - transforming the way in which health care is delivered to meet local needs through the NHS Plan;

  - raising educational standards for all age groups and promoting employment opportunities;

  - reducing crime through an ambitious crime reduction programme and a Ten Year Drug Strategy;

  - improving access to cultural, leisure and sporting activities and using their potential as an educational resource.

- provided substantial extra resources over the next three years to deliver better services in line with those strategies;

- backed the resources with challenging targets set in Public Service Agreements; and

- developed good examples of new models for rejuvenating towns and cities through Urban Regeneration Companies and Millennium Communities.

7.7   To bring about the long-term transformation of our towns and cities action is now needed by everyone:

- **Government:** development and implementation of the new measures and proposals set out here so that there is a full tool kit for urban renaissance;

- **local and regional partners:** continuing to develop regional and local strategies which provide a clear vision within which every town and city can plan for its future;

- **public and private sector bodies, and individuals:** practical projects and activities everywhere from our local streets to the hearts of our great cities so that we create places for people.

Moving forward: the Government's commitment

7.8   The Government is committing itself to a new, long-term partnership with local communities, regional and local bodies, and other key stakeholders including the private sector. The Government will lead and support the overall drive towards better towns and cities.

7.9   To achieve this we will create a new focus for urban issues at the centre of Government and will improve communication and co-ordination with regional and local partners and across government.

7.10   A new Cabinet Committee on Urban Affairs will consider how policies impact on urban areas overall. It will review regularly the implementation of the policies and programmes set out here drawing on advice from the group of Ministers overseeing the Neighbourhood Renewal Unit. It will ensure that the progress in urban areas generally is monitored.

7.11   The Cabinet Committee will have support and advice from two groups to ensure a wider understanding of the state of our cities and the effect of new policies:

  - a new Sounding Board on Urban Issues, bringing together community, academic, professional, private and business interests; and

  - an Urban Sub-group of the Central – Local Partnership (the group which co-ordinates central and local government action generally). This group will also have a specific remit to monitor the implementation of the White Paper.

7.12   As part of the implementation of this White Paper and the action plan for neighbourhood renewal, the Government will ensure that all the agencies for which it is directly responsible will participate fully in the Local Strategic Partnerships and the creation and delivery of Community Strategies. National programmes will respond flexibly to the needs of local communities, thus enabling them to play the fullest possible part in delivering Community Strategies.

7.13   We will create within DETR an Urban Policy Unit, which will support the joint working on the implementation of the White Paper. In addition to civil servants this unit will include staff on secondment from local government and other local partners, and from overseas. We will also invite a number of practitioners and experts in urban policy, from both this country and abroad, to become associate members. This will ensure that we have the benefit of the widest range of experience as we review and develop policies for towns and cities.

7.14 The Urban Policy Unit will work closely with the Neighbourhood Renewal Unit and the Regional Coordination Unit. It will provide the links to the Commission for Architecture & the Built Environment and to the developing resource centres in each region. The Department of the Environment, Transport and the Regions will restructure its objectives to give clear emphasis to the urban dimension of policies.

7.15 Government will now take forward, in consultation with others, the new measures announced here. The chart below sets out the main steps and milestones.

Chart 1 – The way ahead: some key steps and milestones

End 2000	Publication of action plan for neighbourhood renewal
	Housing Policy Statement on taking forward the proposals in the Housing Green Paper, incuding the Starter Home initiative for key workers
April 2001	Increases to main spending programmes start
	Education and Training – including expansion of Excellence in Cities and Sure Start, New Deal for schools, the Learning and Skills Council, free early education for 66% of 3 years olds in areas of greatest need, the Children's Fund and the Excellence Challenge
	Health – continued roll out of the NHS plan; investment in the health service across a wide range of programmes, including a network of Healthy Living Centres
	Jobs – action to remove barriers to work, increase employability and stimulate innovation and enterprise, including enchanced New Deal programmes
	Crime – action to reduce crime and tackle drugs
	Culture, leisure and sporting activity – new creative partnerships for schools, Spaces for Sports and Arts Scheme
	Transport – start of 10 Year Plan, including doubing of funding of Local Transport plans in 2001/02
	Housing – extra investment to improve the condition of social housing comes on line
	RDAs – major increases in funding and increased flexibility to move money between budgets
	Start of programme of work to improve the quality of parks, play-areas and open spaces
By Summer 2001	Finance Act passed confirming package of national fiscal measures to increase investment in urban areas including (subject to practical implications and State Aids rules):
	• exemption from stamp duty for all property transactions in deprived areas
	• accelerated tax relief for cleaning up contaminated land
	• 100 per cent capital allowances for creating 'flats over shops' for letting
	• package of VAT reforms to encourage additional conversion of properties for residential use
	Local Strategic Partnerships in place in the key towns and cities in every region

7

Chart 1 – The way ahead: some key steps and milestones *(continued)*

By Summer 2001 *(continued)*	Consultation on revised PPG1 – General Policy and Principles – to reflect our vision for better towns and cities and for protecting the countryside
	Consultation on review of Planning Obligations – options to include impact fees
	New drive to improve urban regeneration skills through Regional Centres of Excellence
	Five Urban Regeneration Companies identified to bring about the physical transformation of priority areas
	Launch four remaining Millennium Communities
	Launch of City Growth Strategies and Inner City 25
	Local Learning and Skills Councils come into operation
	Enhancement to New Deal Programmes and introduction of a package of measures to reduce barriers to work (including enhancement of Working Families Tax Credit)
	New Higher Education Innovation Fund starts
	New Urban Bus Challenge Fund begins
	Beacon Council Theme on Regeneration through Culture, Sport and Tourism begins
	Local NHS action to tackle health inequalities will be measured and managed through the performance assessment framework
By end 2001	Next stages in development of Local Tax Reinvestment Programme, Town Improvement Schemes and rate relief for small businesses
	New NHS Charter replaces current Patients Charter and proposed changes to clinical governance arrangements for doctors
	Guidance issued on compulsory purchase powers, residential conversions, and bringing empty property back into use
2002	RDA new Single Programme Budget comes into force in full
	Community Strategies in place in the key towns and cities in each region
	Programme to create a People's Network by bringing all public libraries on–line by end-2002; training library staff in ICT and creating tailored content to support life-long learning
	Subject to consultation, first round of new NOF Transforming Communities Programme announced
	Urban Summit hosted by Ministers to celebrate success and ensure action is on track
	By end 2002 all principal councils to have put in operation a new constitution which is transparent, accountable and efficient

7.16 Beginning in Spring 2001 we will publish and maintain, in conjunction with the regional Centres of Excellence and other partners, easily accessible information on all relevant programmes.

Moving forward: local and regional vision

7.17 The diversity of towns and cities means that practical action will depend on the local leadership in each town or city setting out a clear vision and its own action plan within the context of the regional strategy. Developing and agreeing the visions and the strategic action needed will be for local choice influenced by local people with modernised local authorities in the lead.

7.18 Bringing together all the elements of social, economic and physical development to create a new vision for a city will be a complex task requiring imagination and vision. But the experience in major cities such as Manchester and Birmingham has shown that a wide range of partners can come together to identify common goals and work towards them. The early work in a number of areas on the New Commitment to Regeneration (see page 35) to create an overall framework for each area illustrates how the linkages between issues can be identified and proposals developed in a practical way.

7.19 As set out in the Action Plan for the Regional Co-ordination Unit, the Government Offices and other regional partners will ensure that Regional Planning Guidance, Regional Transport Plans and the RDAs' Regional Strategies provide a linked framework giving a clear context for individual towns and cities. In particular the Regional Development Agencies will:

- continue to develop their Regional Strategies and related Action Plans to reflect the increase in resources and the greater freedom they will have to determine how these resources are spent with the transition to a Single Budget;

- participate in Local Strategic Partnerships, especially where the area is a significant strategic priority for the region.

7.20 At local level there is already good progress through the New Commitment to Regeneration and other processes such as Local Agenda 21. This provides the basis for the preparation of Community Strategies through Local Strategic Partnerships. Local authorities will:

- develop Community Strategies in co-operation with the community, service providers, business leaders and other key stakeholders. Working through Local Strategic Partnerships they will want to:

  - assess the strengths and weaknesses of their areas;

  - identify how the policies and programmes that we have summarised in this White Paper can be integrated into an effective Community Strategy;

  - agree action plans with all the service providers and other key stakeholders;

  - agree priorities for action;

  - monitor and chase progress; and

  - contribute to local neighbourhood renewal strategies;

- decide how to use the greater freedom which the single capital pot will give them from April 2002 to deliver better services.

7.21 London remains unique, with some of the characteristics of a region as well as being a city and a key part of the wider South East. The radical new structure of governance in London now has to take up the challenge of the opportunities offered by this White Paper to establish and deliver a vision for our capital city.

London

1. The policies set out in this White Paper are as relevant to London as they are to the rest of the country. But the Government has introduced new and unique arrangements in London – the Greater London Authority, with a directly elected Mayor and Assembly. These will provide strong strategic leadership and restore accountability to London.

2. London's Mayor controls London's new transport and economic development bodies (Transport for London and the London Development Agency), and he appoints the majority of members who sit on the Metropolitan Police Authority and the London Fire and Emergency Planning Authority.

3. The Mayor will prepare strategies for London covering transport, economic development and regeneration, spatial development, bio-diversity, waste management, air quality, ambient noise and culture. All the Mayor's strategies have to be consistent with each other and have to integrate the three cross cutting objectives – sustainable development, health and equality.

4. In addition, the Mayor has general powers to promote economic and social development and the city's environment. In addition to the statutory strategies, the Mayor has decided to produce an energy strategy.

5. The separately elected Assembly acts as a check and balance, with wide-ranging scrutiny powers to investigate issues on behalf of Londoners.

6. The Mayor is responsible for strategic planning for London, and in particular for producing a Spatial Development Strategy (SDS). The SDS offers the opportunity for an integrated approach to shaping the future pattern and direction of development in London.

7. The SDS will include the Mayor's general policies for the development and use of land in London and also incorporate the elements of transport, economic development, environmental and other strategic policies for London, bringing them together in a single, comprehensive framework.

8. As part of the new arrangements, the London Development Agency (LDA) has been created to promote economic development and regeneration in London. It will be responsible for formulating and delivering the Mayor's economic development and regeneration strategy for London.

9. It will work with key London organisations such as the boroughs, businesses, voluntary groups, regeneration partnerships and training institutions and Learning and Skills Councils to deliver the Mayor's economic development strategy. It will manage various funding programmes related to its purposes and carry out regeneration projects where it owns land.

10. Transport for London (TfL) is responsible for many of the transport services in London including the buses, Docklands Light Rail, Croydon Tramlink, the GLA road network and the Underground, once the Public Private Partnership has been agreed. TfL is accountable to the Mayor and responsible for delivering an integrated and sustainable transport strategy.

11. Local and central government remain important in London. The boroughs are responsible for key services such as education. Central government has other key functions such as the National Health Service. So, the framework set out in this White Paper for co-operation through Local Strategic Partnerships will be important in London, to complement the unique London arrangements.

7.22   In some other areas of regional and national importance joint arrangements may be needed. For example, the Thames Gateway area is a priority area for sustainable economic growth. The area suffers from complex structural problems but if development and regeneration are directed effectively it has the potential to make a vital contribution to the wider economy and accommodating the growth of the South East.

7.23   We have therefore established a new Thames Gateway Strategic Partnership led by Ministers to bring together the key bodies responsible for development in the area and provide a cross Gateway focus. The Partnership met for the first time in October and is being supported by a new Thames Gateway Strategic Executive.

Moving forward: places, projects and people

7.24   We are already working with many of the key towns and cities to identify the way forward. Many already have a clear vision of the changes they wish to see in their areas and have plans in place to deliver those changes.

7.25   Within the framework of a clear strategic approach, individual projects and activities need to be developed, designed and implemented. These will depend on local circumstances and needs but will include:

- **small scale projects,** potentially carried out by local people and groups, such as improving a local park or public space, or promoting the renovation of a historic building. Practical small scale action in every neighbourhood is vital to the continuous improvement of the local environment and to fostering the engagement of communities in their future;

- **the identification of areas for concerted action and priority.** These might be town centres, focused around the arrangements needed to carry through Town Improvement Schemes. They might be areas of dereliction with a mixture of land and buildings needing improvement. They might be residential areas needing renewal. They might be areas of sufficient scale and significance to justify a special structure such as an Urban Regeneration Company. In each case local authorities and other public and private partners will need to develop a package of measures and delivery mechansims. This flexible approach of identifying a tailored package and approach develops the proposals by the Urban Task Force for Urban Priority Areas; and

- **new major developments of quality well integrated into the environment.** In many cities the rate of investment through the private sector is increasing. Significant public investment can be expected in buildings and in transport infrastructure. Each of these must be of a high quality in itself; each must be used as the opportunity to improve the wider environment and functioning of the town.

Monitoring the transformation

7.26   This White Paper sets the framework for a process of transformation. We must monitor our progress carefully and be ready to take further steps if need be.

7.27   We have a clear national vision:

A new vision of urban living

Our vision is of towns, cities and suburbs which offer a high quality of life and opportunity for all, not just the few. We want to see:

- **people shaping the future** of their community, supported by strong and truly representative local leaders;

- people living in **attractive, well kept towns and cities** which use space and buildings well;

- good design and planning which makes it practical to live in a **more environmentally sustainable** way, with less noise, pollution and traffic congestion;

- towns and cities able to **create and share prosperity**, investing to help all their citizens reach their full potential; and

- **good quality services** – health, education, housing, transport, finance, shopping, leisure and protection from crime – that meet the needs of people and businesses wherever they are.

This urban renaissance will benefit everyone, making towns and cities vibrant and successful, and protecting the countryside from development pressure.

7.28 Major changes in our towns and cities will be driven forward by the tough targets we have set in the Public Service Agreements for every department. The main relevant targets, with particular emphasis on the most deprived areas, many of which are in cities, are set out in the previous chapters. Overall the main changes will be:

- more jobs by 2004 with the biggest improvements in the 30 areas with the lowest current employment rates and amongst disadvantaged groups;

- reduced crime rates with 30% less vehicle crime by 2004, 25% less domestic burglary by 2005 and 14% less robbery by 2005;

- better education standards in all areas, and in particular in deprived areas, with fewer adults with literacy and numeracy problems, improved GCSE passes and better understanding of ICT and science by 2004;

- better, safer and more reliable transport systems, leading to the increased use of public transport and reductions in road congestion by 2010;

- better housing with all social housing being of a decent standard by 2010 and with most improvement taking place in deprived areas;

- better health services and a reduction in the health gap between the most deprived areas and the rest of the country; and

- a better environment with 60% of new housing provided on previously developed land or through conversions of existing buildings by 2008; 17% of underused land reclaimed by 2010; better designed buildings and places; and clean and more attractive streets.

7.29 The analysis developed in the preparation of this White Paper has illustrated that existing data and indicators do not readily allow for comparisons between various types of urban areas e.g. the conurbation and the freestanding cities or between different parts of the same city e.g. the inner core and the suburbs. This relates closely to the need that Policy Action Team 18 identified for improved small area data to support our understanding of change in neighbourhoods.

7.30 The Urban Policy Unit will collaborate with the Neighbourhood Renewal Unit to ensure that the new small area data being developed under the National Strategy for Neighbourhood Renewal will be able to provide some of the additional information that is needed. They will jointly ensure that an overall picture can be built up from the small area data to describe and track changes in areas of cities and towns, and cities overall. This work will link with further development of the measures in *Quality of Life Counts*, the source for sustainable development indicators published by DETR in December 1999. A project will be undertaken by the ESRC as part of the Cities programme to explore the vialibity of developing a State of the Cities Report modelled on the one carried out by the US Department of Housing and Urban Development.

7.31 In addition to this national work individual towns and cities should ensure that they identify the key areas of change they are seeking and the indicators most relevant to local circumstances. These may be drawn from national data, depend in part on the Best Value measures or be developed as part of the programme of indicators under *Local Quality of Life Counts*, the local handbook published by DETR in July 2000.

7.32 The Urban Policy Unit will complete a review to develop a comprehensive set of key indicators for overall urban analysis by Summer 2001 and the DETR, with interested departments and agencies, will review, establish and promote a standard set of urban and rural definitions for use in analysis and monitoring.

Understanding progress

There are several key sources for the detailed information that will be needed to track progress in every area:

- the annual report of progress against the Public Service Agreement Targets set out in the Spending Review earlier this year;

- the annual report of progress against the 15 headline indicators and selected examples from 147 "Quality of Life" Indicators set out in the UK sustainable development strategy;

- the annual review of performance of local authority services against Best Value indicators; and

- evaluations of the outcomes delivered by individual policies and programmes like Urban Regeneration Companies.

Maintaining the momentum

7.33 The Government through the Urban Policy Unit will be working closely with towns and cities in taking forward the principles in this White Paper. A key focus will be on the most significant cities in each region. We will work with local authorities, RDAs and other stakeholders over the next few months, as they carry forward their planning.

7.34 The first milestone will be an Urban Summit in 2002 hosted by Ministers from across Government. This will consider and celebrate progress by individual towns and cities; ensure that action on policies and programmes is on track; take stock of the evaluations required of this White Paper overall; and identify the need for additional action.

7.35 The second milestone will be a full report on the State of our Cities and Towns in 2005. This will give a comprehensive picture of the progress that has been made toward delivering an urban renaissance in every area.

A long term commitment to action

7.36 This is an ambitious long term programme of change and development in our towns and cities. If places are for people then people must help make the places. The Government has set out its commitment. It will lead the way forward but action will ultimately depend on everyone contributing to change whether as individuals in their own street and neighbourhood, as investors and businesses in shaping the economy of their city, or as local representatives creating the vision for their city.

Places for people (Photograph courtesy of the Association of Town Centre Management)

> *... Cities not only concentrate problems ... but also solutions ... They hold the key to our common future.*
>
> Richard Rogers and Anne Power: Cities for a Small Country

7

Recommendations of the Urban Task Force

The Urban Task Force published their report **"Towards an Urban Renaissance"** in June 1999. The report included 105 recommendations on how to improve our towns and cities. The Government has considered these recommendations carefully in preparing this White Paper and other relevant policy documents. This annex explains in brief how we have responded to each of the Task Force's recommendations and, where appropriate, how we have taken them forward.

Task Force Recommendation	The Government's Response
1. Require local authorities to prepare a single strategy for the public realm and open space, dealing with provision, design, management, funding and maintenance.	See Chapter 4 (paragraph 4.46).
2. Introduce a national programme to create comprehensive green pedestrian routes around and/or across each of our major towns and cities.	*Encouraging Walking*, *Guidance on Full Local Transport Plans* and the revised Planning Policy Guidance note 13 (Transport) promote walking and pedestrian access.
3. Revise planning and funding guidance to: a) Discourage local authorities from using 'density' and 'over development' as reasons for refusing planning permission; b) Create a planning presumption against excessively low density urban development; and c) Provide advice on use of density standards, linked to design quality.	Taken forward in Planning Policy Guidance note 3 (Housing). See Chapter 4 (paragraph 4.24).

Task Force Recommendation	The Government's Response
4. Introduce a mandatory double performance rating for houses combining a single environmental rating, and a single running cost rating, so that house-buyers know what they are getting for their money.	Being taken forward in part in the work on the "House Sellers" pack for speeding up the house buying process. It is proposed that the "Seller's Information Pack" include energy efficiency ratings and advice.
5. Make public funding and planning permissions for area regeneration schemes conditional upon the production of an integrated spatial masterplan, recognising that public finance may be required up front to pay for the masterplanning.	See Chapter 4 (page 50, paragraph 9).
6. All significant area regeneration projects should be the subject of a design competition. Funds should be allocated in any regeneration funding allocation to meet the public costs of such competitions.	The Government has used design competitions for the Millennium Communities programme (see recommendation 8). We would encourage other agencies to use or support design competitions in suitable cases.
7. Develop and implement a national urban design framework, disseminating key design principles through land use planning and public funding guidance, and introducing a new series of best practice guidelines.	To be taken forward in work to revise PPG 1. See Chapter 4 (paragraph 4.26).
8. Building on the millennium communities initiative, undertake a series of government sponsored demonstration projects, adopting an integrated approach to design-led regeneration of different types of urban neighbourhood.	See Chapter 4 (page 49, paragraph 6).
9. Establish local architecture centres in each of our major cities. There should be minimum network of 12 properly funded centres, fulfilling a mix of common objectives and local specialisms.	See Chapter 4 (page 48, paragraph 4).
10. Place local transport plans on a statutory footing. They should include explicit targets for reducing car journeys, and increasing year on year the proportion of trips made on foot, bicycle and public transport.	Being taken forward through Transport Bill 2000 and *Guidance on Full Local Transport Plans. Transport 2010: The Ten Year Plan* also includes targets for bus and light rail use, increasing cycling trips and reducing traffic congestion in large urban areas.
11. Introduce home zones in partnership with local communities, based on a robust legal framework, using tested street designs, reduced speed limits and traffic-calming measures.	See Chapter 4 (page 68, paragraph 1).

Task Force Recommendation	The Government's Response
12. Make public funding and planning permissions for urban development and highway projects conditional on priority being given to the needs of pedestrians and cyclists.	This White Paper, *Transport 2010: The 10 Year Plan* and *Guidance on Full Local Transport Plans* stress the importance of walking and cycling, and the Government would encourage funding and planning bodies to reflect this. The revised Planning Policy Guidance note 13 increases the emphasis given to the needs of cyclists and pedestrians in any future developments.
13. Set targets for public transport within local transport plans that specify maximum walking distances to bus stops; targets on punctuality, use, reliability and frequency of services; and standards for availability of cycle storage facilities at stations and interchanges.	Taken forward in *Guidance on Full Local Transport Plans* and measures under the Transport Bill 2000 to improve bus services in connection with local bus strategies.
14. Extend a well-regulated franchise system for bus services to all English towns and cities if services have not improved substantially within five years.	The Transport Bill 2000 includes the option of area-wide contracting, subject to Ministerial consent.
15. Ensure every low income housing estate is properly connected to the town and district centre by frequent, accessible and affordable public transport.	Being taken forward through *Guidance on Full Local Transport Plans* and Planning Policy Guidance notes 3 (Housing) and 13 (Transport). Also, the Government has recently announced an Urban Bus Challenge which will provide grants to support services to disadvantaged areas.
16. Commit a minimum 65% of transport public expenditure to projects which prioritise walking, cycling and public transport over the next ten years, increased from the current Government estimate of 55%.	*Transport 2010: The Ten Year Plan* and *Guidance on Full Local Transport Plans* set out investment priorities, and stresses the importance of walking, cycling and public transport. But the Government does not propose to set a specific target for the proportion of public expenditure going to particular modes.
17. Give priority to the public transport needs of regeneration areas within local transport plans and public funding decisions.	*Guidance on Full Local Transport Plans* requires public transport needs of regeneration areas to be taken into account. Promoting the renaissance of towns and cities is identified in *Transport 2010 – The 10 Year Plan* as one of the key objectives of the Government's long term transport investment programme.
18. Allow Regional Development Agencies and other regeneration funding bodies to provide funding for transport measures that support their area regeneration objectives.	RDAs may fund transport measures in pursuit of their regeneration and economic objectives. Other regeneration programmes such as New Deal for Communities may also include transport proposals within their plans.

Task Force Recommendation	The Government's Response
19. Set a maximum standard of one car parking space per dwelling for all new urban residential development.	Planning Policy Guidance note 3 advises local authorities that car-parking standards that result, on average, in development with more than 1.5 off-street car parking spaces per dwelling are unlikely to reflect the Government's emphasis on securing sustainable residential environments. This is particularly the case for developments in locations such as town centres where services are readily available by walking, cycling and public transport.
20. Extend plans to tax workplace charging to all forms of private non-residential car parking provision.	Being reviewed by the Commission for Integrated Transport.
21. Provide an above-inflation increase in central resources allocated to local authorities for managing and maintaining the urban environment in each of the next seven years.	The Government has increased funding to local authorities by 3% in real terms over the next 3 years. Grant to local authorities is unhypothecated, so the use of Government funding to support individual services is a matter for local discretion.
22. Assign a strategic role to local authorities in ensuring management of the whole urban environment, with powers to ensure that other property owners, including public utilities and agencies, maintain their land and premises to an acceptable standard.	See Chapter 4 (paragraph 4.46) and subsequent sections.
23. Establish single points of contact within local authorities, which have decision-making authority for the whole range of environmental services devolved to designated estates, neighbourhoods or town centres. In some cases, particularly social housing estates, this should include the appointment of super caretakers or wardens.	The Government agrees that creating a single point of contact within local authorities could be a useful means of improving the way these services are delivered. However, it is for each individual authority to decide how it manages these services. The Government has set up a Neighbourhood Warden Unit to support the development of Neighbourhood Warden schemes and agrees that these can be a useful way of helping to tackle environmental problems. See Chapter 4 (page 71, paragraph 2).
24. Place town improvement zones on a statutory footing, enabling local authorities to work with local businesses to establish jointly funded management arrangements for town centres and other commercial districts.	Currently subject to consultation in *Modernising Local Government Finance: A Green Paper.* See Chapter 4 (page 70, paragraph 5).
25. Pilot different models of neighbourhood management which give local people a stake in the decision-making process, relaxing regulations and guidelines to make it easier to establish devolved arrangements.	Being taken forward through the National Strategy for Neighbourhood Renewal, which will include a programme to pilot neighbourhood management.

Task Force Recommendation	The Government's Response
26. Make public bodies responsible for managing sites blighted by proposed major infrastructure schemes, even where they do not yet own the land. Local authorities should be empowered to take enforcement action if a responsible body reneges on its duties.	Following detailed consideration, the Government does not consider it practical to make public bodies responsible for sites over which they have no rights. Local authorities can take enforcement action against owners who do not maintain sites; and owners of blighted sites may compel the body responsible to purchase them.
27. Strengthen enforcement powers and sanctions against individuals or organisations that breach regulations related to planning conditions, noise pollution, littering, fly-tipping and other forms of anti-social behaviour.	See Chapter 4 (page 71, paragraph 2).
28. Use fines from criminal damage and community reparation to repair and maintain the local environment, according to local people's stated priorities.	The Government has considered this proposal but has concluded that these funds are better spent on resourcing the direct approach to tackling and preventing crime in the first place.
29. Review the performance indicators used by the Audit Commission as they measure standards of management of the urban environment, to produce a more comprehensive and better integrated set of measures.	Taken forward through *Best Value and Audit Commission Performance Indicators 2000/2001 and Best Value and Audit Commission Performance Indicators 2001/2002: Consultation.*
30. Strengthen the New Commitment to Regeneration programme by combining government departments' spending powers to deliver longer-term funding commitments for local authorities and their partners. Central government should be a signatory to local strategies where they accord with national and regional policy objectives.	Taken forward in *Local Strategic Partnerships: Consultation Document*, which builds on the New Commitment approach.
31. Create designated urban priority areas, enabling local authorities and their partners in regeneration, including local people, to apply for special packages of powers and incentives to assist neighbourhood renewal.	The Government agrees with the need to identify areas for concerted action and priority. It considers that the people most qualified to identify these areas are the communities and policy makers on the ground. This White Paper takes a flexible approach to this by identifying a tailored package of measures which can be implemented at the local level.
32. Require regeneration programmes to include a 'hand over' strategy, agreed by the partners, as a condition of funding. The strategy should describe plans for continuity of staff and resources when the funding period is over.	All area regeneration schemes are required to prepare a forward strategy.

Task Force Recommendation	The Government's Response
33. Soften provisions requiring the 'clawback' by government of property sales and other receipts from regeneration programmes, so that a proportion can be re-invested in the long-term management of the area.	The Government will consider waiving "clawback" of receipts where a proposal is made for reinvestment for the benefit of the area.
34. Make it easier for regeneration bodies to endow cash and assets to local trusts and community organisations.	DETR is reviewing the guidance on the endowment of funds to successor bodies. Endowments have already been agreed in particular cases.
35. Enable 'arms-length' urban regeneration companies to co-ordinate or deliver area regeneration projects.	See Chapter 4 (page 62, paragraph 4).
36. Establish housing regeneration companies to undertake regeneration in areas where there is badly deteriorated and vacant stock.	The Housing Corporation is currently examining the feasibility of housing regeneration companies.
37. Introduce special local authority area regeneration committees in urban priority areas, to enhance the quality and speed of decision-making.	It is already possible for local authorities to introduce area regeneration committees. The Local Government Act 2000 and the best value regime strengthen their ability to adapt structures to meet local requirements and assure rigorous monitoring and review.
38. Establish joint working between professional institutions, education providers and employers to develop a plan of action for improving the skills-base in urban development over the next five to seven years.	See Chapter 4 (page 51, paragraph 2).
39. Develop a network of regional resource centres for urban development, promoting regional innovation and good practice, co-ordinating urban development training, and encouraging community involvement in the regeneration process.	See Chapter 4 (page 51, paragraph 2).
40. Establish a five year programme of international secondments – 'Urban 2000' with the aim that at least 2,000 professional staff and trainees benefit from exposure to best practice.	See Chapter 4 (page 51, paragraph 2).
41. Produce detailed planning policy guidance to support the drive for an urban renaissance. This should be backed up by measures to ensure the policies are implemented in regional planning guidance, local development plans, and planning decisions, and enable the full involvement of local communities in the urban planning process.	Taken forward in Planning Policy Guidance note 3 and Planning Policy Guidance note 11 (Regional Planning). The Government has also indicated its commitment to revise Planning Policy Guidance note 1 – see Chapter 4 (paragraph 4.26).

Task Force Recommendation	The Government's Response
42. Strengthen regional planning by enabling regional planning guidance to: a) provide an integrated spatial framework for planning, economic development, housing and transport policies; b) steer development towards more effective use of urban land and buildings accessible by sustainable forms of transport; c) encourage the use of sub-regional plans to set overall requirements for providing housing on brownfield land and in recycled buildings.	Taken forward in the revised Planning Policy Guidance note 11.
43. Simplify local development plans with a stronger emphasis on strategy to create a more flexible basis for planning. The plans should avoid including detailed site-level policies.	Taken forward through Planning Policy Guidance Note 12 (Development Plans).
44. Achieve comprehensive development plan coverage in England by the end of 2002. Where necessary, Government Regional Offices should work alongside under-performing local planning authorities to ensure the deadline is met.	Taken forward through Planning Policy Guidance note 12.
45. Support a more streamlined planning process in urban priority areas by enabling the Secretary of State to take action against authorities that consistently fail to deliver planning permissions within a reasonable time period.	The Government's Modernising Planning Agenda includes initiatives to raise planning performance in all local planning authorities. This is underpinned by authorities' duties under Best Value, which also enables the Secretary of State to take action against those failing to deliver. See Chapter 4 (page 47).
46. Require local planning authorities to conduct a review of all local rules, standards and procedures to consider whether they can be revised or removed to enhance urban development.	Taken forward through Planning Policy Guidance note 3 and *By Design*, the good practice guidance on urban design in the planning system published by DETR and CABE.
47. Devolve detailed planning policies for neighbourhood regeneration, including urban priority areas into more flexible and targeted area plans, based upon the production of a spatial masterplan and the full participation of local people. The resulting policies and guidelines should take the form of strengthened supplementary planning guidance where necessary.	See Chapter 4 (page 47, paragraph 3 and page 50, paragraph 9).
48. Review, at a regional level, the designations of employment sites in local development plans, taking into account economic needs, but avoiding over-provision, and accelerating the release of land for housing development.	Addressed through Regional Planning Guidance.

Task Force Recommendation	The Government's Response
49. Revise and relax national guidance on the use of planning agreements.	To be considered in the forthcoming consultation paper reviewing the current system of planning obligations. See Chapter 4 (page 48, paragraph 6).
50. Establish a 'fast-track' independent arbitration process for the conclusion of Section 106 agreements, which can be triggered by either party after a set period, at their cost.	To be considered in the context of the forthcoming consultation paper reviewing the current system of planning obligations. See Chapter 4 (page 48, paragraph 6).
51. Replace the negotiation of planning gain for smaller urban development schemes, (for example, an end value of less than £1 million), with a standardised system of impact fees. The fees collected should be spent on local environmental improvements and community facilities that reflect the priorities of local people.	To be considered in the context of the forthcoming consultation paper reviewing the current system of planning obligations. See Chapter 4 (page 48, paragraph 6).
52. Review the mechanisms by which local planning authorities use planning gain to secure affordable 'social' housing to ensure that: a) developers have less scope to buy their way out of obligations to provide mixed tenure neighbourhoods; b) local authorities are not obliged to require social housing in contexts where there is already over-provision in that neighbourhood.	Taken forward in Planning Policy Guidance note 3. Research into the use by local planning authorities of their powers to seek affordable housing contributions has been commissioned and good practice guidance will be published next year.
53. Enable more mixed income housing projects to proceed, including use of more challenging planning briefs and discounted equity stakes for low to middle income households in areas where property values are high.	Taken forward through Planning Policy Guidance note 3 and the Green Paper *Quality and Choice: A Decent Home for All*. PPG3 encourages a greater mix of dwellings and greater quality of choice to help promote social inclusion.
54. Establish clear procedures under the proposed 'plan, monitor and manage' system for assessing future housing demand, to ensure the early correction of an emerging under-supply or over-supply of housing.	Taken forward though Planning Policy Guidance notes 3 and 11 and Regional Planning Guidance. See Chapter 4 (paragraph 4.24).
55. Oblige all local planning authorities to carry out regular urban capacity studies on a consistent basis, as part of their development plan-making process, where necessary working together across borough boundaries.	Taken forward through Planning Policy Guidance note 3. See Chapter 4 (paragraph 4.24).

Task Force Recommendation	The Government's Response
56. Formally adopt a sequential approach to the release of land and buildings for housing, supported by a system of regional and sub-regional reconciliation of housing needs and demand. Planning guidance should specify monitoring procedures for every local planning authority to apply.	Taken forward through Planning Policy Guidance notes 3 and 11.
57. Set ambitious targets for the proportion of new housing to be developed on recycled land in urban areas where housing demand is currently low.	The national target is that by 2008, 60% of additional housing should be provided on previously developed land and through conversions of existing buildings.
58. Require local authorities to remove allocations of greenfield land for housing from development plans where the allocations are no longer consistent with planning policy objectives.	Taken forward through Planning Policy Guidance note 3.
59. Retain the general presumption against development on designated Green Belt. Review whether there is a case for designating valuable urban green space in a similar way.	See Chapter 4 (page 44, paragraph 4.24, page 74, paragraph 2 and page 76).
60. Provide information on the regeneration potential of land and building assets in future editions of the National Asset Register.	To be addressed by the forthcoming update of the National Asset Register.
61. Introduce a statutory duty for public bodies and utilities with significant urban landholdings to release redundant land and buildings for regeneration. Regional planning bodies could monitor compliance with the new duty and whether targets for land release are being met.	The Government does not propose to legislate to compel private sector organisations to release redundant land for regeneration. Management of Government owned vacant dwellings taken forward in Chapter 4 (page 56, paragraph 5). Compulsory Purchase Order powers are available where a case for compulsory purchase can be made.
62. Require organisations such as the Ministry of Defence and NHS Estates to negotiate the transfer of portfolios of development land to Regional Development Agencies and local authorities to secure locally determined regeneration objectives.	Public sector organisations will be given greater incentive to dispose of redundant land by the move to resource accounting which will result in their bearing the full economic costs for all assets retained.
63. Consider options for reflecting the full environmental costs of new development through the use of economic instruments. Particular attention should be given to the feasibility of introducing a system of environmental impact fees through the planning system.	To be addressed in the forthcoming consultation paper reviewing the current system of planning obligations.

Task Force Recommendation	The Government's Response
64. Prepare a scheme for taxing vacant land, which does not penalise genuine developers, but which deters owners holding onto land unnecessarily.	The Government does not, at this stage, propose to introduce a scheme for taxing vacant land as we do not think that it would be effective in ensuring that vacant land is brought into use. Chapter 4 sets out a large number of measures we are introducing to encourage the reuse of vacant land.
65. Strengthen and increase local authority powers of foreclosure and enforced sale to provide speedy mechanisms for dealing with abandoned and dilapidated sites or buildings.	The Government proposes to issue best practice guidance on ways in which local authorities can lay a charge against private land where they have had to incur costs in cleaning it up. The Government also proposes to issue best practice guidance to local authorities on the use of powers to clean up land adversely affecting the amenity of a neighbourhood. See Chapter 4 (page 71, paragraph 2).
66. Modify the general development order so that advertising, car parking and other low-grade temporary uses no longer have deemed planning permission on derelict and vacant land.	The Government does not consider that amending the order along the lines suggested would be the right way forward.
67. Allow local authorities and other public bodies flexibility to pay disturbance payments over and above market value in reaching negotiated settlements for the acquisition of land. They should also be able to make greater use of purchase options and deferred acquisition payments.	Local authorities can make such payments, if they are satisfied that they can be justified.
68. Create revolving funds for land assembly, so that public investment in the initial costs of site purchase can be off-set by a share of subsequent gains achieved through regeneration and disposal.	Regional Development Agencies through the Land and Property budget are already assembling and disposing of sites and recycling the receipts for further regeneration projects.
69. Streamline and consolidate compulsory purchase order (CPO) legislation. In the meantime, reinforce positive legal decisions on the powers of local authorities by amending the relevant Government guidance.	Being taken forward in the current review of laws and procedures relating to compulsory purchase, compensation and the disposal of compulsorily purchased land. The Government has made a commitment (Chapter 4, page 59, paragraph 5) to bring forward proposals for legislation when Parliamentary time allows.
70. Assist the land assembly process in urban priority areas by removing the obligation for authorities to prove a specific and economically viable scheme when making compulsory purchase orders. They should, however, still be required to prove the potential for creating long-term development value in the site.	Being taken forward in the current review of laws and procedures relating to compulsory purchase, compensation and the disposal of compulsorily purchased land.

Task Force Recommendation	The Government's Response
71. Allow an additional 10% above market value to be payable as compensation for the compulsory purchase of all properties. Payment of the extra compensation should be tapered according to a timetable to encourage early settlement.	Being taken forward in the current review of laws and procedures relating to compulsory purchase, compensation and the disposal of compulsorily purchased land.
72. Resolve conflicts and inconsistencies between the environmental regulation systems, covering contaminated land, water and waste at the first legislative opportunity. Site owners should only have one set of standards to work to when resolving problems of site contamination.	See Chapter 4 (page 60).
73. Establish an Environment Agency 'one stop shop' service for regulatory and licensing requirements, moving quickly to a position where a single regeneration licence is available covering all the regulatory requirements for cleaning up a site.	The Government will consider the need for a 'one stop shop' as part of the debate on options for the future control of land remediation.
74. Give landowners greater assurances that the regulators are unlikely to take future action over contaminated sites once remediation schemes have been carried out to an agreed standard.	The Government does not think it appropriate for regulators to give an assurance that they will not take any further action at a particular site. This would be a significant departure from the polluter pays principle.
75. Establish a national framework for identifying, managing and communicating the risks that arise throughout the assessment, treatment and after-care of contaminated and previously contaminated sites.	See Chapter 4 (page 60).
76. Pilot standardised land condition statements, to provide more certainty and consistency in the management and sale of contaminated and previously contaminated land.	A consortium of organisations has recently completed work on a new land condition record. See Chapter 4 (page 60, paragraph 5).
77. Launch a national campaign to 'clean up our land.' Targets should be set: a) for the net reduction of derelict land over the next 5, 10 and 15 years; b) to bring all contaminated land back into beneficial use by 2030.	The Spending Review 2000 has set a performance target that: 60% of new housing should by 2008 be provided on previously developed land and through conversion of existing buildings. Brownfield land will be reclaimed at a rate of over 1,100 hectares per annum by 2004 (reclaiming 5% of current brownfield land by 2004 and 17% by 2010). The Government has also announced that it intends to introduce accelerated payable tax credits for cleaning up contaminated land. See Chapter 4 (paragraph 4.10).

Task Force Recommendation	The Government's Response
78. Enforce a regime of strict liability on site owners who add to the problem of contaminated land, drawing on Integrated Pollution Control and Integrated Pollution Prevention Control regulations.	The Government strongly agrees that liability for any land contamination must lie with those that caused it. There is a robust system of environmental controls to prevent new contamination already in place.
79. Give local authorities a statutory duty to maintain an empty property strategy that sets clear targets for reducing levels of vacant stock. There should be firm commitments to take action against owners who refuse to sell their properties or restore them to beneficial use.	Local authorities are required to measure their performance in bringing empty homes back into use. We do not think it is necessary to impose a statutory duty on them, but we will continue to work with the Empty Homes Agency and others to support local authorities in this area. See Chapter 4 (page 56).
80. Allocate social housing by a more open system than just a strict need to be accommodated. In unpopular areas, available housing should be marketed to other groups, including low to middle income working households and students.	Being taken forward through *Quality and choice: A Decent Home for All.*
81. Introduce new measures to encourage the restoration and use of historic buildings left empty by their owners. These should include revised planning guidance (PPG15), inclusion of heritage issues in regional economic strategies, a review of building regulations and an end to the business rate exemptions on empty listed buildings.	The Government will consider these issues in the light of the forthcoming report from English Heritage on the historic environment. The Government has announced that it is attracted to reducing VAT for listed buildings that are places of worship and has written to the European Commission to make its position clear. See Chapter 4 (page 72, paragraph 5).
82. Review and enhance the role of civic amenity societies in planning the re-use of historic buildings and in securing regeneration objectives.	The Government agrees that amenity societies should play an active role in issues affecting the re-use of historic buildings and in securing regeneration objectives. Representatives of the Joint Committee of Amenity Societies are involved in the current review of heritage policy. See Chapter 4 (page 72, paragraph 4).
83. Facilitate the conversion of more empty space over shops into flats by providing additional public assistance, including public equity stakes and business rate reductions.	As announced in the November 2000 Pre-Budget Report the Government intends to introduce in Budget 2001 an £80m package of measures to encourage property conversions. This includes a tax relief to property owners for the costs of converting redundant space over shops and other commercial premises into flats for letting. See Chapter 4 (paragraph 4.10).

Task Force Recommendation	The Government's Response
84. Harmonise VAT rates at a zero rate in respect of new building, and conversions and refurbishments. If harmonisation can only be achieved at a 5% rate, then a significant part of the proceeds should be reinvested in urban regeneration.	See reference in Chapter 4 (paragraph 4.10). As announced in the November 2000 Pre-Budget Report, the Government intends to introduce a package of targeted VAT reforms to encourage additional conversion of properties for residential use including: • A reduced 5% rate of VAT for the cost of converting residential properties; and • An adjustment to the zero rate of VAT to provide relief for the sale of renovated houses which have been empty for 10 years or more. The Government is also attracted to the idea of offering a reduced rate of VAT for the repair and maintenance of listed buildings used as places of worship and has written to the European Commission to make its position clear. The Government has no plans to change the tax base.
85. Extend liability for full payment of Council Tax to all owners of empty homes. Where properties have been empty for over a year, the authority should have discretion to impose a higher charge.	The Government does not propose to introduce such a change to Council Tax liability at this stage.
86. Establish a ten year national programme – The Renaissance Fund – to help repair our towns, whereby community groups and voluntary organisations can access the resources needed to tackle derelict buildings and other eyesores that are spoiling their neighbourhood.	See Chapter 4 (page 71, paragraph 4).
87. Establish national public–private investment funds that can attract an additional £1 billion in private investment for area regeneration projects over the next three years. A minimum of 50% of the resources should be directed at residential portfolios.	See Chapter 4 (page 63, paragraph 8).
88. Introduce regional regeneration investment companies and funds, to increase the amount of private finance flowing into the regeneration of all the English regions.	The Government has announced a new target umbrella fund to build on the regional venture capital funds and others. £100m of public funds have been allocated as a stimulus to lever in private sector funding. The Government is also supporting the development of a number of new ways to attract long term private investment in regeneration. See Chapter 4 (page 62). The Government's response to the Social Investment Task Force report is set out in Chapter 5 (page 96, paragraph 5).

Task Force Recommendation	The Government's Response
89. Pilot an estate renewal project and a more general area regeneration project through the private finance initiative.	Being taken forward through *Quality and Choice: A Decent Home for All.*
90. Introduce a new financial instrument for attracting institutional investment into the residential private rented market.	While the Government would like to see increases in the level of institutional investment in the residential private rented market it is not persuaded of the case for introducing this financial instrument.
91. Introduce a package of tax measures, providing incentives for developers, investors, small landlords, owner-occupiers and tenants to contribute to the regeneration of urban sites and buildings that would not otherwise be developed.	The November 2000 Pre-Budget Report announced that the Government would introduce a substantial package of measures with a cumulative Exchequer cost of £1 billion over 5 years in response to these recommendations. These complement and build on the measures we have already put in place to revive our most disadvantaged communities. Details of the package are set out in paragraphs 6.74-6.85 of the Pre-Budget Report. They are also discussed in Chapter 4 (paragraph 4.10).
92. Include the objective of an urban renaissance in the terms of reference for the 2001 comprehensive spending review which will determine public expenditure priorities for the following three years.	The Spending Review 2000 made urban renaissance a priority. It provides significant new resources for improving public services such as education and tackling crime. It also allocated additional resources to regeneration programmes, including the strengthening of the role of the RDAs and the first steps to implementing the National Strategy for Neighbourhood Renewal through the Neighbourhood Renewal Fund and through a refocused New Deal for Communities.
93. Amend the Public Service Agreements set for government departments to include urban renaissance objectives. A single 'urban renaissance public service agreement' should be developed to operate across Whitehall following the 2001 spending review.	Being taken forward through the establishment of "Floor Targets" in the Spending Review 2000. These will ensure that everybody can expect a minimum level of public services, a key contribution to an urban renaissance.
94. All significant public buildings should be subject to a design competition, adequately funded by the public purse.	The Government has established a Ministerial Champion for good design in each department and encourages local authorities and others to commission competitions for public buildings where appropriate.
95. Review the spending formula used to allocate central resources to local government so that it adequately reflects the financial needs of urban authorities in managing and maintaining their areas.	A major review of the method used to distribute grants amongst local authorities has been carried out. Options for reforming the method of distributing grant are set out in *Modernising Local Government Finance: A Green Paper*. Also, the new Neighbourhood Renewal Fund provides £800m to fund improvements to deprived areas.

Task Force Recommendation	The Government's Response
96. Extend Government commitments to capital finance allocations against local spending strategies so they go beyond the definite plans of the three Public Expenditure Survey years.	The future arrangements for local authority capital finance are discussed in *Modernising Local Government Finance: A Green Paper.*
97. Independently review the funding allocations, policies and formulas for school buildings, to produce proposals for accommodating future increases in pupil numbers in high quality facilities in regenerating urban areas.	Being taken forward through the Government's proposed schools capital strategy.
98. Allow local authorities to retain a proportion of additional revenue generated from council tax and business rates as a result of regeneration in designated urban priority areas. The retained resources should be recycled into the management and maintenance of the area.	Currently subject to consultation in *Modernising Local Government Finance: A Green Paper* and referred to in Chapter 4 (page 63, paragraph 12).
99. Combine the single regeneration budget challenge fund and most of the land and property funding inherited from English Partnerships to create a single regional funding pot for area regeneration.	The Spending Review 2000 significantly increased the resources for RDAs. Their combined budget will rise from £1.2 billion this year to £1.7 billion in 2003/04. The Spending Review also announced the introduction of a Single Programme Budget for the RDAs starting in April 2002. See Chapter 5 (page 81, paragraph 25-27).
100. Give Regional Development Agencies (RDAs) the freedom to establish flexible area regeneration funding programmes over ten years or more, with a clear funding bank established for the full period.	The Government will be introducing greater budgetary flexibility for the RDAs from April 2001 as a transitional arrangement prior to the introduction of the single programme budget in April 2002. See Chapter 5 (page 81, paragraph 25-27).
101. RDAs should offer a 'one-stop shop' project appraisal service for applicants that cuts across requirements of individual funding programmes.	The Government and the RDAs are looking at how application procedures could be simplified and the appraisal system made more transparent.
102. Commission an independent review of the National Lottery's impact on urban regeneration, focusing on its potential distorting effects on priorities, and on how appraisal, monitoring and delivery can be better co-ordinated with other agencies.	DCMS is planning a wide evaluation of the economic and social impact of the National Lottery.

Task Force Recommendation	The Government's Response
103. Introduce a package of measures, including some debt cancellation, to enable local authorities with large social housing portfolios to transfer some or all of the stock to arms-length management organisations.	Being taken forward through *Quality and choice: A Decent Home for All.*
104. Restrict public subsidy for social housing developments of more than 25 homes to schemes where homes for rent are integrated with shared and full-ownership housing.	The Government is adopting a flexible approach where the scope for mixed tenure development is considered for all schemes of over 25 homes but not imposed in unsuitable areas.
105. Increase the cost effectiveness of public support for housing renewal by private owners by using a mix of grants, loans, equity stakes and tax relief to encourage home improvements.	Being taken forward through *Quality and Choice: A Decent Home for All.*

Bibliography

Chapter 1

1991 Census; Office for Population and Census Statistics; 1992

English House Condition Survey 1996; DETR; 1998

Ethnic Minorities in Britain; Modood et al; PSI; 1997

Labour Force Survey 1998-1999 Annual Data; ONS; 2000

Living in Urban England: Attitudes and Aspirations; DETR; 2000

Our Countryside: the Future – A Fair Deal for Rural England; DETR; November 2000

Population Trends 100: Summer 2000; ONS; The Stationery Office; 2000

The State of English Cities; Brian Robson, Michael Parkinson, Martin Boddy, Duncan Maclennan; DETR; 2000

Towards an Urban Renaissance; Urban Task Force; E&FN Spon; June 1999

Urbanisation in England: Projections 1991 – 2016; ONS; HMSO; 1995

Chapter 2

1991 Census; Office for Population and Census Statistics; 1992

Annual Employment Survey 1999; ONS; 2000

A Better Quality of Life: A Strategy for Sustainable Development for the United Kingdom; DETR; The Stationery Office; May 1999

Health Survey for England: Cardiovascular disease 1998; Department of Health; The Stationery Office; 1999

Indices of Deprivation 2000; Michael Noble et al, Oxford University; DETR; 2000

The Jobs Gap in Britain's cities: Employment loss and labour market consequence; Ivan Turok and Nicola Edge; Policy Press; 1999

Labour and Life of the People in London; Charles Booth; 1889-1903

Living in Urban England: Attitudes and Aspirations; DETR; 2000

'Outward Migration: a threat to urban development?' Tony Champion; Cityscape, ESRC; Autumn 1999

Population Trends 100: Summer 2000; ONS; The Stationery Office; 2000

Projections of Households in England to 2021; DETR; October 1999

The State of English Cities; Brian Robson, Michael Parkinson, Martin Boddy, Duncan Maclennan; DETR; 2000

Towards an Urban Renaissance; Urban Task Force; E&FN Spon; June 1999

Chapter 3

All Our Futures: The Report of the Steering Committee of the Better Government for Older People Programme; Cabinet Office; The Stationery Office; June 2000

Draft Code of Guidance for Local Authorities on the Allocation of Accommodation and Homelessness; DETR; April 1999

Fairness at Work White Paper Cm 3968; DTI; HMSO; May 1998

Guide to Quality Schemes and Best Value; DETR; February 2000

Local Strategic Partnerships: Consultation Document; DETR; October 2000

Local Public Service Agreements: A Prospectus for Local Authorities; DETR; July 2000

Modern Local Government: In Touch with the People Cm 4014; DETR; 1998

Modernising Local Government Finance: A Green Paper; DETR; 2000

National Strategy for Neighbourhood Renewal: a framework consultation; Social Exclusion Unit; The Stationery Office; 2000

Report of the Stephen Lawrence Inquiry; Sir William MacPherson of Cluny; The Stationery Office; February 1999

Chapter 4

The 2000 British Crime Survey: England and Wales, Home Office Statistical Bulletin 18/00; Home Office; The Stationery Office; 2000

The Building Act 1984; DETR; HMSO; 1984

The Building Act 1984: Building Regulations Proposals for Amending the Energy Efficiency Provisions: A Consultation Paper issued by Building Regulations Division, DETR; June 2000.

The Building Act 1984, The Building Regulations 1991, Approved Document to Part M, Access and Facilities for Disabled People, Transitional Provisions in the Building Regulations Amendment Regulations 1998; DETR; The Stationery Office; 1998

Building a Better Quality of Life: A Strategy For More Sustainable Construction; DETR; April 2000

Building Control Performance Standards; DETR; 1999

By Design, Urban Design in the Planning System: Towards Better Practice; DETR; May 2000

Civilising Cities: The contribution of transport and land use: Phase one report; RAC Foundation, Civic Trust, CSS; RAC Foundation; 1998

Code of Practice on Litter and Refuse; DETR; The Stationery Office; 1999

The Control of Fly Posting: A Good Practice Guide; DETR; The Stationery Office; November 2000

DETR Circular 02/2000: Environmental Protection Act 1990 Part II A: Contaminated Land; The Stationery Office; March 2000

Fundamental Review of the Laws and Procedures relating to Compulsory Purchase and Compensation: Final Report; DETR; July 2000

The Heritage Dividend: Measuring the Results of English Heritage Regeneration 1994-99; English Heritage; 1999

Living in Urban England: Attitudes and Aspirations; DETR; 2000

Local Housing Needs Assessment: A Guide to Good Practice; DETR; 2000.

Low Demand Housing and Unpopular Neighbourhoods; G Bramley, H Pawson, and H Third; DETR; 2000

Modernising Planning: A Policy Statement by the Minister for the Regions, Regeneration and Planning; DETR; 1998

Monitoring Provision of Housing through the Planning System: Towards Better Practice; DETR; October 2000

National Land Use Database; http://www.nlud.org.uk/; DETR/English Partnerships/Ordnance Survey/IDeA; Ongoing

People's Panel; Telephone Wave 3 for DETR; April 1999

Planning for Communities of the Future Cm 3885; DETR; February 1998

Planning Policy Guidance note 3: Housing; DETR; The Stationery Office; March 2000

Planning Policy Guidance note 6: Town Centres and Retail Development; DoE; The Stationery Office; June 1996

Planning Policy Guidance note 12: Development Plans; DETR; The Stationery Office; December 1999

Planning Users' Concordat; Local Government Association; LGA Publications; 2000

Population Trends 100: Summer 2000; ONS; The Stationery Office; 2000

Rethinking Construction – The Report of the Construction Task Force; DETR; July 1998

Strategic Sites Database; www.englishsites.com

Streets as Living Space; Carmen Hass-Klau; Landor Publishing; 1999

Survey of English Housing, 1995/96; DETR; The Stationery Office; 1997

Sustainable Urban Extensions: Planned Through Design; The Prince's Foundation, DETR, English Partnerships and CPRE; The Prince's Foundation; September 2000

Tomorrow's Roads – Safer for Everyone; DETR; March 2000.

Towards an Urban Renaissance; Urban Task Force; E &FN Spon; June 1999

Town and Country Parks Report of the Environment, Transport and Regional Affairs Committee; House of Commons; November 1999.

Urban Design Compendium; English Partnerships and the Housing Corporation; English Partnerships; August 2000

Urban Regeneration Companies: A Process Evaluation; DETR; 2000

Chapter 5

'The 1998/99 Labour Force survey: Annual Local Area Database' in **Labour Market Trends**; D. Burke; ONS; April 2000

Enterprising Communities – Wealth Beyond Welfare: A Report to the Chancellor of the Exchequer; The Social Investment Task Force; UK Social Investment Forum; 2000

European Cities Monitor; Healey and Baker; 1998

Excellence and Opportunity: A Science and Innovation Policy for the 21st Century Cm 4814; DTI; The Stationery Office; 2000

The Global Entrepreneurship Monitor: 1999 UK Executive Report; London Business School; 1999

Good Policy Making: A Guide to Regulatory Impact Assessment; Better Regulation Unit; Cabinet Office; 2000

Pre-Budget Report; HM Treasury; The Stationery Office; November 2000

'Inner City 100', Inc. Magazine, May 2000, Vol 22 Issue 6; Inc Magazine; 2000

Transport 2010: The 10 Year Plan; DETR; 2000

UK Tourism Survey 1999; English Tourism Council; 2000

Chapter 6

Bringing Britain Together: A National Strategy for Neighbourhood Renewal Cm 4045; Cabinet Office; The Stationery Office; September 1998

The 2000 British Crime Survey; Chris Kershaw, Tracey Budd, Graham Kinshott, Joanna Mattinson, Pat Mayhew and Andy Myhill; Home Office; October 2000

The Crime and Disorder Act 1998; HMSO; 1998

English House Condition Survey 1996; DETR; 1998

The Health Act 1999; HMSO; 1999

Housing Policy and Practice; Peter Malpass and Alan Murie; MacMillan/Palgrave; April 1999

Indices of Deprivation 2000; Michael Noble et al, Oxford University; DETR; 2000

Labour Force Survey – monthly statistics; DfEE; ONS; 2000 (monthly issues)

Local Public Service Agreements: A Prospectus for Local Authorities; DETR; July 2000

Local Strategic Partnerships: Consultation Document; DETR; October 2000

Living in Urban England: Attitudes and Aspirations; DETR; 2000

Modern Local Government: In Touch with the People Cm 4014; DETR; July 1998

NHS Plan Cm 4818; Department of Health; The Stationery Office; July 2000

National Strategy for Neighbourhood Renewal: A framework for consultation; Social Exclusion Unit; The Stationery Office; April 2000

Neighbour nuisance, social landlords and the law; Caroline Hunter, Judy Nixon and Sigrid Shayer; Chartered Institute of Housing; July 2000

The Neighbourhood Renewal Fund: Consultation Paper; DETR; October 2000

Neighbourhood Warden Schemes: An overview. Crime Reduction Research Series Paper 2; Jessica Jacobson and Esther Saville, Home Office; 1999

Policy Action Team Reports 1-18; Various Government Departments, co-ordinated by Cabinet Office Social Exclusion Unit; The Stationery Office; 1999 – 2000

Planning Out Crime: Circular; DoE; DETR (ex DoE); March 1994

Projections of Households in England to 2021; DETR; October 1999

Prudent for a Purpose: Building Opportunity and Security for All Spending Review 2000 – New Public Spending Plans 2001 – 2004; Her Majesty's Treasury; 2000

The State of English Cities; Brian Robson, Michael Parkinson, Martin Boddy, Duncan Maclennan; DETR; 2000

Quality and Choice: A Decent Home for All – The Housing Green Paper; DETR, DSS; April 2000

Chapter 7

Best Value and Audit Commission Performance Indicators for 2000/2001; DETR; December 1999

A Better Quality of Life: A Strategy for Sustainable Development for the United Kingdom; DETR; The Stationery Office; May 1999

The 2000 British Crime Survey: England and Wales, Home Office Statistical Bullertin 18/00; Home Office; The Stationery Office; 2000

Cities for a Small Country; Richard Rogers and Anne Power; Faber; 2000

Local Quality of Life Counts: A handbook for a menu of local indicators of sustainable development; DETR; July 2000

Public Services for the Future: Modernisation, Reform; Accountability – White Paper on Public Services Cm 4181; Cabinet Office; The Stationery Office; March 1999

Quality and Choice: A Decent Home for All – The Housing Green Paper; DETR, DSS; April 2000

Urban Regeneration Companies: A Process Evaluation; DETR; October 2000

Printed in the UK for The Stationery Office Limited
On behalf of the Controller of Her Majesty's Stationery Office
Reprinted 12/00 with corrections
Dd5069693 12/00. 25038, TJ003233